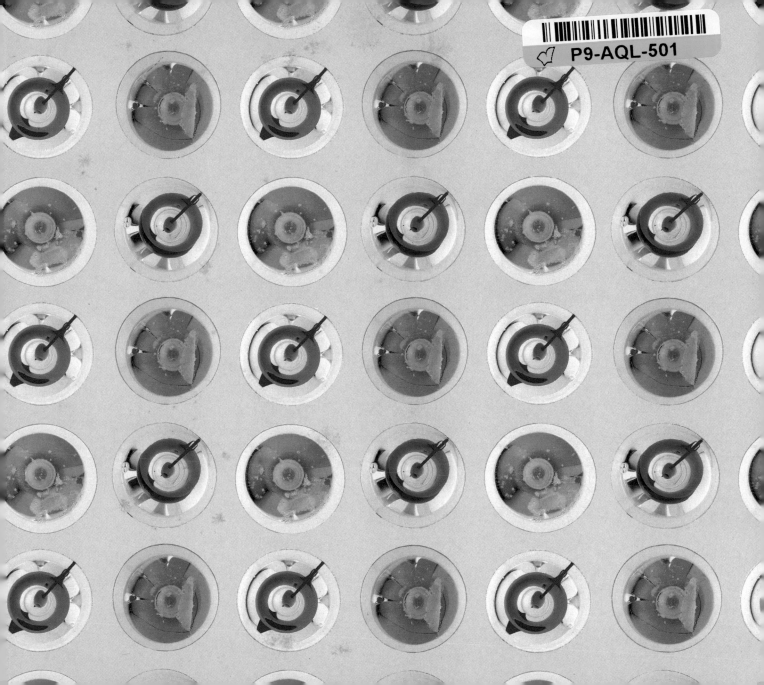
P9-AQL-501

Tanqueray®

THE PERFECT ENTERTAINER

BEV BENNETT & KIM UPTON

A COLLECTION OF RECIPES FOR COCKTAILS, CANAPES & HORS D'OEUVRES

BARRON'S

Woodbury, New York • London • Toronto • Sydney

All inquiries should be addressed to:

Barron's Educational Series, Inc.
113 Crossways Park Drive
Woodbury, New York 11797

International Standard Book No. 0-8120-5772-4

PRINTED IN THE UNITED STATES OF AMERICA
6 7   9 7 7   9 8 7 6 5 4 3 2 1

Color photography by Matthew Klein
Food stylist, Andrea Swenson
Prop stylist, Linda Cheverton

Accessories courtesy of the following:
China from Villeroy and Boch, Inc.,
41 Madison Avenue, New York City
Crystal and silverware from Royal Copenhagen/
Georg Jenson, 683 Madison Avenue, New York City
Flowers by Ann Titus
Handthrown porcelain from Gordon Foster,
1322 Third Avenue, New York City.

Jacket and cover design by The Sukon Group, Inc.
Book design by Milton Glaser, Inc.

Tanqueray Gin

The Life of the Best Parties

It should come as no surprise to connoisseurs of fine spirits that Tanqueray's beginnings are as aristocratic as its reputation! David, the first Tanqueray in England, was a French emigre whose artistry with precious metals earned for him the title "Official Goldsmith" to King Charles II in the early eighteenth century. Charles, his direct descendent, inherited his passion for excellence, but his ambitions took a different turn. He formulated the first recipe for quality gin in England using the waters from the Finsbury Spa, the purest in all of England. He distilled and redistilled his spirit to his own exacting requirements. He flavored it with an exclusive and secret formula, a combination of herbs and botanicals. The year was 1830. The rest is history.

The formula was an instant success among a select, distinctively British clientele, and soon after, Tanqueray was exported to the Colonies. With its future launched, the success of the spirit in the distinctive green bottle was simply a matter of time, not to mention taste.

Tanqueray arrived in America in the 1950's, where it was adopted enthusiastically by the Hollywood crowd. But its appeal was so compelling that within a few years it spread east.

Today, Tanqueray is enjoyed in more than 100 countries, but the United States is by far its largest market. The familiar green bottle is a fixture on the bars of our best homes, restaurants and bars. Charles Tanqueray's original recipe remains unchanged, and is the company's most treasured secret.

Tanqueray has been described as smooth as English silk, dry as Shaw's wit; in short, the perfect gin. We invite you and your guests to enjoy the best of parties with the best of gin.

Tanqueray Gin

CONTENTS

Thanks to Barbara Roth, Virginia Motan,
Jeff Bredenberg, J. Linn Allen, George Jewell,
and our editor, Carole Berglie.

INTRODUCTION

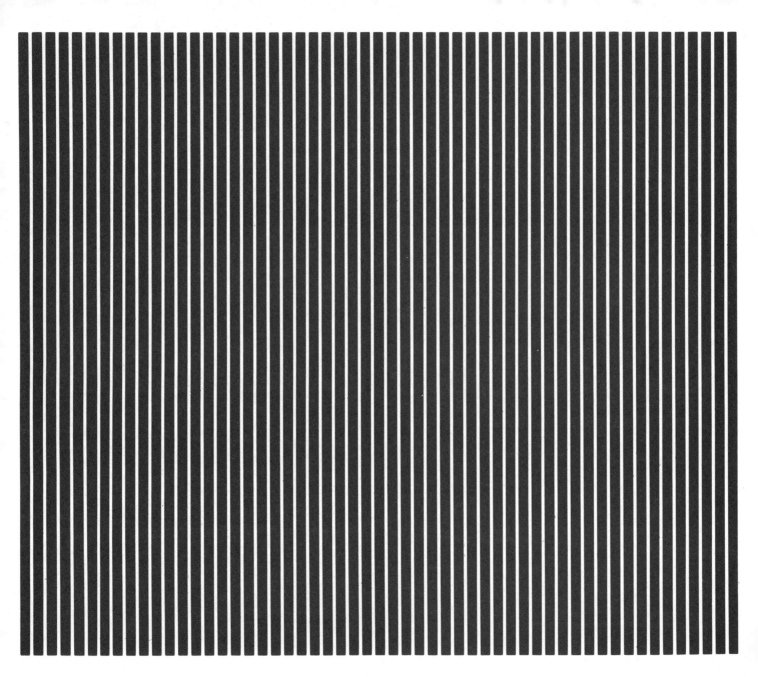

here are many occasions for which a cocktail party is more appropriate than a dinner. Among them are any celebration called with two hours' notice, any event to which you would like to invite more guests than you have dishes for, any occasion for which you do not want to serve an entire meal, and any party planned with the express purpose of showing off clothing that wrinkles when you sit.

It is a simple event capable of serving multiple purposes. Perhaps that is why it's so popular.

Loosely defined, a cocktail party is a gathering at which cocktails, wine, beer, and nonalcoholic beverages are served. They are accompanied by foods that may be eaten without a knife, fork, or spoon. They are for the betterment of mankind through good conversation and food. They are supposed to be fun.

A cocktail party should be a gathering of friends numbering from two to two hundred. It should celebrate food in its finest rather than greasiest forms. It should offer dishes meant as snacks but good enough for sit-down dinners.

It should create joy for the host as well as the guests. Except for early morning, when even people of good cheer find socializing second only to discussing taxes as a ridiculous form of behavior, you can schedule a cocktail party any time and any place that adults feel comfortable congregating.

The invitation, whether oral or written (written is better, because it offers physical proof of your intention and acts as a reminder to you that the house should be cleaned), must be specific. It should include where the party is to be held; a phone number to which guests may direct questions, responses and excuses; the day of the week the party is to be held, the date, and the time (beginning and ending); clothing requirements (for example, "black tie not required" or "no one will be served unless he is wearing shoes and shirt"); and the fact that the event will be celebrated with cocktails and hors d'oeuvre *only*. This last statement is of the utmost importance. Imagine inviting sixty marathoners for a snack after the big race only to have them appear with appetites primed for dinner.

Despite their casual appearance, cocktail parties are bound by certain rules. We have mentioned several, but perhaps the most important rule often goes unsaid. That rule is that the host should, for the sake of his guests, have a marvelous time at the party himself.

Even a potentially smashing celebration can be spoiled if the person hosting it appears to have spent the day scrubbing floors. While there's a good chance this may be the case, guests should not have to think of such things while they are trying to enjoy themselves. The best way to give guests the impression that you are happy, excited, and well rested is to be that way. The way to accomplish this is to prepare ahead, and not bite off more than you can chew, physically or figuratively.

Getting Started

Planning a menu mere mortals can handle is the key.

Beginning a week or two before the party, if time permits, create a menu that combines complementary flavors, appearances, cooking techniques, and preparation times, taking into account the number of people to be served and whether they are adventuresome or cautious regarding new foods.

On separate lists, write the ingredients necessary to create each dish, the ingredients necessary for each beverage, and the serving piece in which each food and beverage is to be presented.

Next plot out the shopping and preparation necessary for each dish and drink. Follow this like a map when preparing for your party.

4

The menu may include several breads and crackers, commercially prepared or homemade. Most of the offerings in our chapter on breads (Not the Yeast of Them), may be baked in advance and frozen.

To serve, wrap the breads in foil and reheat. Guests may think the breads have been freshly baked. Do not correct this misconception.

With the breads, offer a compound butter such as Garlic-Parsley Butter, Hot Anchovy Butter, Orange Honey Butter, or a good-quality plain butter.

Select one or more recipes from our chapter Foods That Come in from the Cold— foods that are "cooked" in the refrigerator. These must be made in advance and refrigerated to reach peak flavor. Marinated Green Olives, for example, may be made several weeks in advance; they improve the longer they are allowed to sit.

For visual effect, select one or more foods from the chapter called Spectaculars. These dishes also are dramatic as a first course at a sit-down dinner.

Relatively quick-to-make foods (from the chapter Fast Takes) can be assembled without much fuss and make good ballast for any cocktail party. Several may be made in advance and refrigerated, including Almost Fish Tartare, Hummus in Red Pepper Shells, Tapenade Tomatoes, and Nuts for Apricots.

It probably is wise to include only one deep-fried food at a party, because such foods must be cooked just before serving.

Beverages should reflect the nature of the food (for example, white wine if the food is light, beer and tequila or gin if it is spicy). At minimum, beverages probably should include a nonalcoholic drink, a beer of some kind, wine, one or two alcohols such as whiskey and vodka, and several mixers.

Remaining menu items should balance kinds of foods (fowl, beef, seafood, and vegetables) with preparation styles from our chapters on pastry-wrapped foods (The Wrap Up), foods that are cooked in the oven or broiler (Not Half-Baked), and dishes that require stove-top cooking (Foods That Pan Out). Many of these (Ratatouille Lemons, Chutney Eggs, and New Potatoes Tonnato) must be made in advance.

Above all, the menu should be an interesting blend of flavors (spicy, subtle, salty, garlicky), textures (smooth, crunchy, chewy), and colors. Visually, it should be a celebration.

Personal serving pieces in a variety of shapes can help the table look nice. They also can act as an aid in starting conversation. Flowerpots, baskets, pails, bird cages (without birds), bottles, bricks and memorabilia such as children's toys all can successfully and even humorously take up residence on a cocktail buffet table. Greens (lettuce and plants included) almost always make food look attractive. Flowers lend an air of festivity.

Tablecloths transform even card tables into lovely serving arenas. But if the table is to be endowed with a wide variety of foods, keep the cloth covering simple. Deer and antelope may be a nice touch for a simple dinner (especially if children and hunters are present), but a tablecloth bearing their likenesses could give a cocktail party the air of a zoo.

Choose a cloth that will enhance the food, not distract from it.

If the food should be visually interesting, it can be intellectually interesting, too. Themes are not necessary, but they help in planning.

A summer party could center on foods that are served cold or tepid. The menu might include Cheese Terrine with Pinenuts and Strawberries, A Salmon Caper, Tapenade Tomatoes, Asparagus in the Pink, Gingered Sausage, and Pesto Pull-Apart Bread.

A menu of Asian foods could include two recipes recently gleaned from our travels in India: Indian Pepper Bread and Kashmiri Spiced Meatballs. Add several sushis, Egg Rolls with Slightly Sour Apricot Sauce, Tandoori Chicken, Marbled Tea Eggs, or Pork Satay with Peanut Sauce, and you have a sampling of cooking styles and spices from all over Asia.

With only a few hours' notice, you can put together a party with Pear Truffles, Steamed Broccoli with Gorgonzola Mayonnaise, Saganaki (flaming cheese), Barbecued Chicken Wings, Scallops in Remoulade Sauce, Bagna Cauda, a selection of breads, and butter.

An hors d'oeuvre table with a Mexican and South American bent could feature Sea Scallop Escabeche with Sichuan Peppercorns, Guacamole, Messy Nachos, Southwestern Pecans, Tomato Salsa with Orange, Chili Bread Sticks, Chorizo Fingers, and Corn Crêpes.

For a party that must be prepared several days in advance, plan to serve Chicken Liver

Pâté, Braided Whole Wheat Molasses Bread, An Appetizer Cheesecake Inspired by Maida Heatter, Gravlax, and Layered Torte in a Hollowed-Out Bread.

A seafood buffet could include Shrimp Boil with Garlic-Chili Mayonnaise, Steamed Mussels, Papaya or Melon Draped in Smoked Salmon, Scallops in Pea-Pod Beds, fresh vegetables, Fried Oysters, Steamed Red Snapper, and Skewered Snails Wrapped in Bacon.

To further ensure that you will enjoy your own cocktail celebration, ALWAYS schedule one hour of quiet time before a party. This can be used for a nap, a hot bath, or, if appropriate, a trip to the baby-sitter's. And it will help you switch gears from preparation of food to presentation of yourself.

Be Prepared

Among the puzzles of planning an hors d'oeuvre party is determining how much food to serve. Our advice is to provide more food than you think necessary—perhaps seven or eight pieces per person—assuming that if flavors are interesting enough people will allow themselves to overindulge. Our recipes offer guidance with serving amounts.

Determining the amount of alcohol to be served is not quite as easy. Generally, though, you can figure on at least one drink per person per hour. This applies to beer, alcohol, and wine. The exception to this rule is Champagne, which people seem capable of drinking in practically unlimited quantities.

Most sensible people will happily drink Champagne from a paper cup, and we certainly would not criticize because it is almost impossible to harm Champagne, except by letting it go flat.

But Champagne is perhaps best suited to a fluted Champagne glass that is tall, thin, and stemmed. It allows the bouquet to glide gracefully to the nose at the same time the Champagne is being tasted by the mouth.

7

Little equipment is necessary for setting up a good bar. Nice, but not essential are a jigger (1½ ounces) measuring glass, measuring spoons, a citrus squeezer, a shaker for quickly blending and cooling without diluting with too much ice, an ice bucket, and—for drinks in which you want crushed ice—a blender. Absolutely necessary, unless your wine has a screw top, is a corkscrew.

Basic glassware may include an Old-Fashioned glass (6 to 8 ounces) which can be used for anything from a Manhattan to a Whiskey Sour to a Bloody Mary; a 4-ounce Martini Glass, which can be used for Tanqueray Martinis, Margaritas or Daiquiris, and a 10-ounce tall Collins glass, which is appropriate for Tanqueray and tonic as well as soft drinks.

A Pilsner glass is fun for beer, especially if it's frosted by submerging in water, then placing in the freezer for a while before using. A stemmed mug can be used for just about any hot drink, and a brandy snifter makes a good Brandy or Cognac taste even better. A stemmed wine glass is useful for Sangria, Champagne, Mimosa, Spritzer, and Kir.

Certainly, having glassware that is appropriate for each drink is the hallmark of a well-stocked bar. But there is no substitute for a well-prepared drink, even if that drink is served in a paper cup. A good drink, like good food, begins with good quality alcohol and mixer.

The best quality alcohol and mixers are the products you believe to be the best tasting. Should you question your own tastes, you can get guidance from consumer magazines and newspapers that occasionally assemble panels of experts to sample several different brands of the same product. The library can provide such articles. Asking the opinions of friends also can be helpful. Fortunately, no decisions are necessary when it comes to finding the proper lime or lemon juice. With rare exceptions, fresh is best.

A well-stocked bar should include good-quality vodka, Tanqueray gin, Johnnie Walker Scotch, bourbon, whiskey, light and dark rum, red and white wines, tequila, sweet and dry vermouth, Triple Sec, soft drinks, and other nonalcoholic beverages, tonic, bitters, club soda, lime and lemon juices, lime and lemon wedges, lots of ice cubes, and several kinds of beer. Buy a reduced-calorie beer, a domestic beer, and one or two imports such as a dark European beer and a Mexican, Asian, or Canadian beer.

Stocking your pantry and freezer can be almost as easy as stocking your bar. Anyone who believes forearmed is forewarned can entertain guests at almost a moment's notice if the refrigerator and freezer contain puff pastry, pastry dough, Southwestern Nuts, Tomato Salsa with Orange, eggroll wrappers, crêpe shells, cream cheese, crackers and cocktail bread, butter, herbs, spices, a selection of cheeses and greens to line a serving platter or basket.

Puff pastry can be wrapped around a wedge of cheese that has been spread with fruit preserves. Baked on a foil-lined cookie sheet in a 425-degree oven for 20 minutes, the pastry will turn golden and the cheese melted and creamy.

Defrosted pastry dough can be pressed into muffin tins and baked in a 400-degree oven for a few minutes until it begins to color. It can be filled with cheddar cheese and sliced green olives, and baked in a 350-degree oven until the cheese melts.

Southwestern Nuts can be served almost straight from the freezer. They take only a minute to defrost. Tomato Salsa with Orange will keep for weeks in the refrigerator and is delicious with commercially prepared corn chips.

Eggroll wrappers can be filled with just about anything and, once deep-fried, taste terrific.

A combination of several kinds of cheese served with fruit, butter, bread, and crackers on a platter or in a basket lined with greens makes an impressive snack because it is visually appealing, delicious, and because you can snatch it from your refrigerator and serve it quickly.

In Conclusion

As any host knows, the best guest is one who leaves before the food supply has been depleted, yet not before the host is in the mood for peace. This is a tricky moment requiring a form of intuition that is seldom taught.

It is appropriate for the host to offer some signal that is easily understood yet not so obvious as turning off the lights. Our suggestion is for the host to (with some pomp) bring out coffee and Chocolate Truffles with Hazelnut Liqueur.

Guests will sink their teeth into the only creamy sweet of the event, recognize it as dessert, and instantly realize that the party has been smashing but that it is time to depart.

If this doesn't work, perhaps you had better turn out the lights.

Opposite: Layered Torte in a Hollowed-out Bread (recipe on page 47). Following page: Cheese Terrine with Pinenuts and Strawberries (recipe on page 50); and Kir (recipe on page 23).

DRINKS

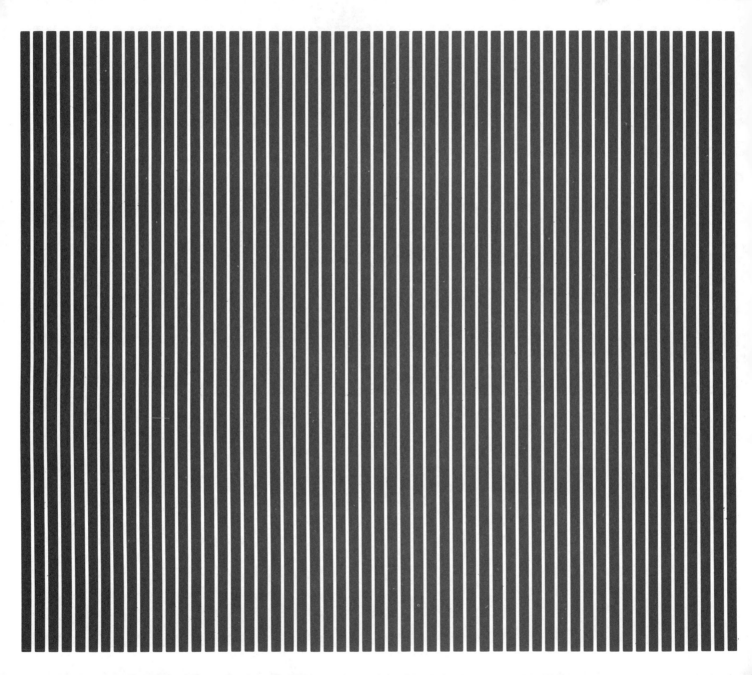

Anything wet, served from a glass and not resembling a milkshake is an appropriate drink for a cocktail party.

If you have someone tending bar, say, someone like Nick "Thin Man" Charles, your guests can indulge in our perfectly made Manhattan, Martini, or the heady combination of Scotch and Drambuie called a Rusty Nail.

However, if your guests have to fend for themselves, make a pitcher of drinks and set them out on the bar.

White or Red Sangria; One, Two, Three Rum Punch; or a Bloody Mary are all marvelous during the summer. To take the chill off a cold party, make a batch of Mulled Cinnamon Cider, Hot Red Wine with Cloves and Almonds, or Irish Coffee. Keep the brew in an insulated jug.

Sugar Syrup

As many beginning bartenders know, granulated sugar takes forever to dissolve in a drink. It settles in a pool at the bottom, which means the beginning of a cocktail is bitter, the end overly sweet (though less offensive than the reverse).

To get around this, prepare a sugar syrup. Combine water with twice as much sugar in a small saucepan. Bring to a boil and swirl the pan to dissolve the sugar. Cool the mixture, and use it to sweeten drinks.

As an example, 4 tablespoons of sugar and 2 tablespoons water will make ¼ cup sugar syrup.

A Brief Guide to Alcohol

Bitters: Herb, root, or bark-flavored spirits, of varying low alcoholic content. These spirits are called bitters because of their taste and should be used sparingly as an accent to a drink.

Bourbon: A distilled whiskey from a mash of at least 51 percent corn.

Brandy: A distilled wine. The category includes the high-quality French Cognac and Armagnac. Germany, Italy, Spain, and America also produce fine brandies. When using brandy in a fruity mixed drink, choose what is inexpensive, but still potable. When buying brandy to serve straight, select what you think tastes best.

Gin: A subtle to assertive-flavored alcohol made from the distillation of grain spirits, then accented with juniper berries and herbs. Each manufacturer has his own gin formula, and every gin-producing country, a particular style. Gin's taste will vary according to the country of origin as well as the liquor company.

Liqueur: A wide variety of drinks generally defined as a combination of spirits, sugar, and herbs, plants, or fruits. The flavoring is the predominant feature of each liqueur.

For example, Grand Marnier has an orange taste and can be used in mixed drinks where a sweet orange flavor is desirable. Apricot liqueur will provide a fruity apricot taste. Drambuie, made from Scotch whiskey, herbs, and honey, lends a slightly sweet, slightly woodsy note to a drink.

Rum: a sugarcane-based spirit that ranges in color from clear to amber and, in taste, from delicate to full bodied. When substituting rum for gin or vodka in light mixed drinks such as Rum and Tonic or a Rum Screwdriver, choose the clear product. For fruit punches, select a dark rum.

Scotch: A malt whiskey that can be just as complex and just as heady a drink as brandy. Serve Scotch plain, with water, club soda, or perhaps with Drambuie in a Rusty Nail. Don't use it for punch.

Sherry: A fortified wine to which brandy has been added. It's a light drink with an alcoholic content of about 16 percent.

Tequila: A colorless distilled alcohol from a Mexican cactuslike plant. Tequila is the foundation of a Margarita, but can also be used in place of vodka in many mixed drinks.

Vermouth: A combination of wine, herbs, and flavorings. Like sherry, vermouth has a low alcoholic content, about 16 percent. It is used as an aperitif or as an accent to many drinks and especially the Martini. Vermouth can be dry or sweet, so check the label.

Whiskey: As general a category as wine, but for a distilled grain product. Whiskey can be Irish, Scotch, Canadian, or American, which includes bourbon, corn whiskey, and rye whiskey.

Cocktail Confidence

Once you understand the basic formula for the most popular drinks, you can vary the type of alcohol and proportions to suit your taste. For a guide to glass shapes and sizes, see pages 212–213.

Here are some definitions that should help.

Cocktail: Usually made with one of the standard liquors—Tanqueray gin, vodka, or whiskey — and flavored with an onion, olive, vermouth, or bitters.

Collins: A tall, refreshing drink of Tanqueray, vodka, or rum mixed with lemon or lime juice, usually sweetened with confectioners sugar and diluted with club soda.

Fizz: A long, sparkly drink of Tanqueray or vodka, lemon juice, syrup, club soda, and ice.

Flip: As nourishing as an alcoholic beverage can get, this drink contains wine or brandy with sugar, nutmeg, and an egg. It's mixed with shaved ice to make it frothy.

Frappe: Alcohol, such as crème de cassis, poured over shaved ice. This is a snow cone for adults.

Highball: A basic alcohol, often whiskey, combined with club soda or another mixer and plenty of ice.

Punch: A mixture of alcohol, fruit, sweetener, and sometimes a mixer. It's prepared in batches and served hot or cold, depending upon the recipe.

Sling: A tall mixed drink that usually starts with Tanqueray and includes sugar, fruit juice, and sometimes a liqueur.

Sour: Whiskey, bourbon, or brandy sometimes sweetened with sugar syrup and flavored with lemon, lime or orange juice.

Iced Chili Vodka with Lemon Peel

Minted Sake

● 1 JALAPEÑO CHILI	● FRESH CORIANDER SPRIGS
● ZEST OF ½ LEMON	(CILANTRO)
● 1 BOTTLE (25 OZ)	
GOOD-QUALITY VODKA	

Want to set the world or at least your tongue on fire? Iced Chili Vodka is best if made with the highest-quality vodka available, but it also does wonderful things for the less expensive brands. Those who like their taste buds tingling may want to leave the chili in longer than the recipe recommends.

1 Quarter chili but do not remove the seeds. Add chili pieces and lemon zest to vodka, place in freezer, and allow to marinate for 2 to 4 hours or until vodka reaches the desired degree of hotness. It will get hotter as it marinates.

2 Strain out chili and lemon peel and serve very cold over ice, garnished with sprigs of coriander.

SERVES 6 TO 8

● 1 PINT (2 CUPS) SAKE	● ¼ CUP FRESH MINT LEAVES

Minted Sake is the perfect accompaniment for sushi of any kind. But don't stop there. It pairs well with seafood too.

1 In a small saucepan, heat sake and mint until hot but not boiling. Turn off heat, cover, and allow to steep for 5 minutes.

2 Remove mint and serve either hot or very cold.

SERVES 4

Mulled Cinnamon Cider

● ½ GALLON APPLE CIDER	● ZEST OF 1 ORANGE
● 6 CINNAMON STICKS	● RUM (OPTIONAL)
● 1 TBSP WHOLE CLOVES	● CINNAMON STICKS
● 2 TBSP ALLSPICE BERRIES	

Mulled Cinnamon Cider is one of our favorite cold-weather drinks. Gently spiced with cloves and cinnamon, it fills the house with a lovely fragrance while it simmers.

1 In a large saucepan, combine cider, cinnamon sticks, cloves, allspice, and orange zest. Bring to a boil. Turn heat down, cover tightly, and simmer 15 minutes.

2 Sieve mixture into mugs. Add 1 ounce (2 tablespoons) of rum to each mug, if desired. Garnish each mug with a cinnamon stick. Serve hot.

MAKES ABOUT 8 (1-CUP) SERVINGS

Bloody Mary

● 1 LARGE CAN (46 OZ) TOMATO JUICE	● 2½ OZ (⅓ CUP) LEMON JUICE
● 2 OZ (¼ CUP) WORCESTERSHIRE SAUCE	● HOT PEPPER SAUCE
	● VODKA
● 3 TBSP PREPARED HORSERADISH	● FRESHLY GROUND BLACK PEPPER
● 2½ OZ (⅓ CUP) LIME JUICE	● FRESH HERB SPRIGS

1 In a large saucepan combine tomato juice, Worcestershire, horseradish, lime and lemon juices, and hot pepper sauce to taste. Bring to a boil. Turn off heat. Refrigerate until cold.

2 Add 1½ ounces vodka—3 tablespoons—(or to taste) to each ½ cup tomato juice. Serve over ice, sprinkle with pepper, and garnish with herbs.

SERVES 12

Ginger Vodka

● 1 PINT (2 CUPS) VODKA	● LEMON WEDGES
● 1 PIECE (2 IN.)	● SUPERFINE SUGAR
GINGERROOT, PEELED	(OPTIONAL)

1 Combine vodka and ginger in a glass jar. Cover tightly and store at room temperature, 2 to 3 days, shaking occasionally. Strain and discard ginger.

2 To serve, pour 2 ounces (¼ cup) Ginger Vodka into a Martini glass. Either squeeze in juice from lemon wedge or just garnish with wedge. If desired, sweeten drink with 1 teaspoon superfine sugar per serving.

SERVES 8

Mimosa

● 2 OZ (¼ CUP)	● 1 ORANGE SLICE
ORANGE JUICE, CHILLED	
● 4 OZ (½ CUP)	
CHAMPAGNE, CHILLED	

1 Pour orange juice into a tall, generous glass. Then fill the glass with Champagne.

2 Garnish with an orange slice.

SERVES 1

Red Sangria

Spritzer

● 1 BOTTLE DRY RED WINE	● 1 ORANGE, CUT INTO 8
● 2 OZ (¼ CUP) GRAND	WEDGES
MARNIER OR OTHER	● 1 LEMON, CUT INTO 8
ORANGE-FLAVORED	WEDGES
LIQUEUR	● 1 CUP CLUB SODA
● 1 TBSP SUPERFINE SUGAR	

● 4 OZ (½ CUP) RHINE WINE	● 1 LIME WEDGE
OR OTHER FRUITY WHITE	
WINE, CHILLED	
● 4 OZ (½ CUP) PLAIN OR	
LIME-FLAVORED CLUB	
SODA, CHILLED	

A well-made sangria should be fruity, refreshing, and slightly potent, as this recipe is. It's the adult answer to overly sweetened punches.

1 Mix wine, Grand Marnier, and sugar in a carafe. Add orange and lemon wedges. Chill up to 24 hours.

2 Just before serving, add club soda and ice cubes.

SERVES 6

Spritzers are a summertime party favorite. Don't bother searching for a dry white wine; fruity is better.

1 Pour wine into tall, full glass. Add club soda and lime wedge.

2 Add 2 to 3 ice cubes and serve immediately.

SERVES 1

Our Favorite Manhattan

● 1 OZ (2 TBSP) SWEET	● 4 DROPS BITTERS
VERMOUTH	● 1 MARACHINO CHERRY
● 1 OZ (2 TBSP)	(OPTIONAL)
GOOD-QUALITY BOURBON	
WHISKEY	

1 Combine vermouth, bourbon, bitters, and ice in a glass. Stir for a few seconds to cool.

2 Pour drink into Old-fashioned glass, straining out ice if desired. Garnish with a cherry.

SERVES 1

The Margarita

● LIME JUICE	● ¼ TO ½ TSP
● COARSE SALT	CONFECTIONERS SUGAR
● 1½ OZ (3 TBSP) TEQUILA	(OPTIONAL)
● ½ OZ (1 TBSP) COINTREAU	● 1 LIME WEDGE
● 1 OZ (2 TBSP) LIME JUICE	

1 Dip the rim of a stemmed Martini glass into lime juice and then into salt, so that rim is coated with salt. Set aside.

2 Combine tequila, Cointreau, lime juice, and sugar, if using. Add ice and stir for a few seconds to cool. Strain out ice and pour drink into salt-dipped Martini glass. Garnish with lime, if desired.

SERVES 1

A Daiquiri

● 2 OZ (¼ CUP) WHITE RUM	● 1 TSP SUGAR SYRUP (PAGE 13)
● ¾ OZ (1½ TBSP) LIME JUICE	

1 Combine rum, lime juice, and sugar syrup with ice. Stir to cool.

2 Pour drink into a stemmed cocktail glass, straining out ice. Add cubes or crushed ice, if desired.

SERVES 1

Irish Coffee

● 1 CUP HOT COFFEE	● SEVERAL DROPS OF MINT EXTRACT (OPTIONAL)
● 1 TSP SUGAR	
● 1½ OZ (3 TBSP) IRISH WHISKEY	● SWEETENED WHIPPED CREAM

1 Pour hot coffee into a stemmed mug that has a handle. Add sugar and stir for a few seconds until sugar is dissolved.

2 Add whiskey and mint extract, if using. Top with a generous dab of whipped cream and serve immediately.

SERVES 1

Hot Red Wine with Cloves and Almonds

● 1 QT (4 CUPS) DRY RED WINE	● ½ CUP RAISINS
● 4 OZ (½ CUP) VODKA	● ¾ CUP BLANCHED ALMONDS
● 4 OZ (½ CUP) BRANDY	● ¼ CUP SUGAR
● 2 CINNAMON STICKS	● 1 SLICED ORANGE
● ½ TSP WHOLE CLOVES	

A cold or damp day is the perfect time for Hot Red Wine with Cloves and Almonds.

1 In a large saucepan, combine red wine, vodka, brandy, cinnamon sticks, cloves, raisins, almonds, sugar, and orange slices. Heat until hot but do not boil. Let sit with heat turned off for 15 minutes.

2 Reheat but do not boil. Sieve into mugs and garnish with an orange slice.

SERVES 6 TO 8

Kir and Kir Royal

● 1 TSP CRÈME DE CASSIS (BLACK CURRANT LIQUEUR)	● 1 THIN SLICE OF LEMON ZEST
● 4 OZ (½ CUP) DRY WHITE WINE (FOR KIR) OR CHAMPAGNE (FOR KIR ROYALE)	

1 In a wine glass (for Kir) or a Champagne flute (for Kir Royale), pour in the crème de cassis and add white wine or Champagne.

2 Garnish with lemon zest and then serve immediately.

SERVES 1

Gin and Tonic

Gimlet

● 2 OZ (¼ CUP) **TANQUERAY**	● 6 OZ (¾ CUP) TONIC,
GIN	CHILLED
	● 1 LIME WEDGE

● 1 TBSP SUGAR SYRUP	● 2 OZ (¼ CUP) **TANQUERAY**
(PAGE 13)	GIN OR VODKA
● ½ OZ (1 TBSP) LIME JUICE	● 1 LIME WEDGE

In the following recipe, the flavor of Tanqueray gin comes through. Those who prefer a less assertive taste can reduce the amount of gin.

1 Pour Tanqueray gin into a highball glass. Add ice.

2 Pour in tonic and garnish with lime. Serve immediately.

SERVES 1

1 In a shaker, combine sugar syrup, lime juice, and Tanqueray gin or vodka. Add 2 or 3 ice cubes and stir well.

2 Strain mixture into Martini or Champagne saucer glass. Garnish with lime. Serve very cold.

SERVES 1

White Sangria

● 4 OZ (½ CUP) CHENIN	● ½ MEDIUM-SIZE ORANGE
BLANC OR OTHER FRUITY	● 2 OZ (¼ CUP) CLUB SODA
WHITE WINE	(OPTIONAL)
● ½ OZ (1 TBSP) GRAND	
MARNIER	

1 Combine wine and Grand Marnier in a tall wine glass. Cut orange into chunks and add chunks to the glass. Chill.

2 If desired, add club soda just before serving. Serve cold.

SERVES 1

Whiskey Sour

● 1 TBSP SUGAR SYRUP	● 2 OZ (¼ CUP) WHISKEY
(PAGE 13)	● 1 ORANGE SLICE
● 1½ OZ (3 TBSP)	
LEMON JUICE	

1 Combine sugar syrup, lemon juice, and whiskey. Pour into Old-fashioned glass and add ice.

2 Garnish with orange slice. Serve cold.

SERVES 1

Martini

Mint Julep

● 2 OZ (¼ CUP) **TANQUERAY** GIN	● 1 OLIVE OR TWIST OF LEMON
● ¼ TSP DRY VERMOUTH	

● 1 TBSP SUGAR	● 2 OZ (¼ CUP) BOURBON WHISKEY
● ¼ OZ (½ TBSP) WATER	
● 6 FRESH MINT LEAVES	● 1 MINT SPRIG

Some claim the secret to the perfect dry martini is to let Tanqueray gin and dry vermouth bottles share cabinet space for six months. Others suggest having a sip of dry vermouth and breathing onto a glass of Tanqueray gin. Our secret is to keep things very, very cold.

1 Place a shaker in the freezer for 1 hour before beginning. Place Tanqueray gin in shaker with vermouth. Add 2 or 3 ice cubes. Stir well, then strain into Martini glass.

2 Either drop in an olive or dangle a twist of lemon on the rim of the glass. Serve very cold.

SERVES 1

This drink is fast becoming a spring ritual around Kentucky Derby time. Instead of using the traditional squat pewter or sterling julep cups, one hostess we know asks her guests to bring their old baby cups.

1 Combine sugar and water in a small saucepan. Bring to a boil and stir to dissolve sugar. Remove from heat and add mint leaves. Stir well and chill.

2 Place julep cup (if julep cup isn't available, use Old-fashioned glass) in freezer for 30 minutes.

3 Remove mint leaves from sugar mixture. Place 1 teaspoon sugar mixture in chilled cup. Add bourbon and stir well. Fill the cup with ice and garnish with the mint sprig. Serve cold.

SERVES 1

Opposite: Tanqueray Martini. Following page: An Appetizer Cheesecake (recipe on page 52).

Black Velvet

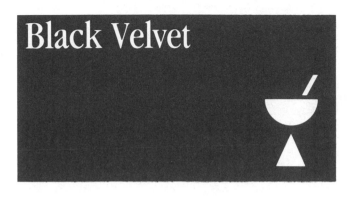

● 4 OZ (½ CUP) GUINNESS	● 4 OZ (½ CUP)
STOUT, CHILLED	GOOD-QUALITY
	CHAMPAGNE, CHILLED

This drink is excellent with spicy, hot foods as an alternative to wine or beer.

1 Pour stout into a tall, generous glass.

2 Fill with an equal amount Champagne. (Pour Champagne and stout along the side of the glass for a smaller head of foam.) Serve immediately.

SERVES 1

Tanqueray Orange Aid

● 4 OZ (½ CUP) ORANGE	● 1 OZ (2 TBSP) GRAND
JUICE	MARNIER
● 1 TBSP SUGAR SYRUP	● CLUB SODA
(OPTIONAL; PAGE 13)	
● 2 OZ (¼ CUP) TANQUERAY	
GIN OR VODKA	

More sophisticated than a screwdriver, more flavorful than a Collins, Orange Aid rescues a simple orange cocktail.

1 In a tall glass, stir together orange juice and syrup. Add Tanqueray gin and Grand Marnier and stir. Add ice and stir again.

2 Fill glass with club soda. Serve cold.

SERVES 1

Opposite: Tandoori Kebabs (recipe on page 49); and Black Velvet. Preceding page: Buckwheat Crêpes with Caviar (page 54).

Rusty Nail

● 1 OZ (2 TBSP) SCOTCH	● 1 OZ (2 TBSP) DRAMBUIE
WHISKEY	● DASH OF BITTERS

1 Combine Scotch, Drambuie, and bitters in an Old-fashioned glass.

2 Add ice; stir and serve cold.

SERVES 1

Bacardi Cocktail

● ½ OZ (1 TBSP) LIME JUICE	● ½ TSP GRENADINE
● 1 TSP SUGAR SYRUP	● 2 OZ (¼ CUP) WHITE RUM
(PAGE 13)	● LIME SLICE

1 Combine lime juice, sugar syrup, grenadine, and rum in a shaker. Stir well and add ice. Shake vigorously.

2 Strain into a Martini glass and garnish with a lime slice. Serve cold.

SERVES 1

One, Two, Three Rum Punch

Bourbon Sour

● 1 OZ (2 TBSP) FRESH LIME	● 2 OZ (¼ CUP) DARK RUM
JUICE	● ½ CUP CLUB SODA OR
● 1 TBSP SUGAR SYRUP	ORANGE JUICE
(PAGE 13)	● ¼ CUP CHAMPAGNE
● 1 OZ (2 TBSP) APRICOT	(OPTIONAL)
BRANDY	

● 1 OZ (2 TBSP) BOURBON	● ¼ TO ½ CUP CLUB SODA
● 1 OZ (2 TBSP) APRICOT	(OPTIONAL)
BRANDY	
● ½ TO 1 OZ (1 TO 2 TBSP)	
LEMON JUICE	

There are three ways to serve this cocktail, each equally refreshing. First mix the basic drink ingredients. For a light drink, finish the recipe with club soda. For something fruity, add orange juice instead. For something bubbly and fruity, add both the orange juice and Champagne.

1 Place lime juice, sugar syrup, apricot brandy, and rum in a tall glass. Stir well. Add ice.

2 Fill with either club soda or orange juice. If opting for orange juice, the Champagne can be added as well.

SERVES 1

This drink is slightly sweet, slightly tart, and very potent. It makes a lasting impression at a cocktail party.

1 Combine bourbon and apricot brandy in an Old-fashioned glass.

2 Stir in lemon juice. Add club soda if desired, and add 1 or 2 ice cubes.

SERVES 1

Rob Roy

● 2 OZ (¼ CUP) SCOTCH	● 1 MARASCHINO CHERRY
WHISKEY	
● ½ OZ (1 TBSP) SWEET	
VERMOUTH	

For some reason this drink seems very popular around Christmas. Perhaps it's the festive red cherry garnish, or the warming power of Scotch.

1 Stir Scotch and vermouth well with ice.

2 Strain into a chilled Martini glass and top with cherry.

SERVES 1

Note

Use a light Scotch whiskey for this drink. For a slightly sweeter, herbal flavor use 1½ ounces Scotch (3 tablespoons) and ½ ounce (1 tablespoon) Drambuie with the same amount of vermouth.

Fruit Sangria with Almonds

● 24 OZ (1 PINT, 8 OZ)	● 1 TSP WHOLE CLOVES
WHITE GRAPE JUICE	● GRAPES
● 1 ORANGE, SLICED	● STRAWBERRIES
● 1 TSP ALMOND EXTRACT	
● 2 TBSP SLICED BLANCHED	
ALMONDS	

1 In a large saucepan, combine grape juice, orange slices, almond extract, almonds, and cloves. Bring to a boil. Turn off heat and chill. When very cold, strain out orange, almonds, and cloves.

2 To serve, fill a wine glass half full of grapes and cleaned but not hulled strawberries. Pour in Fruit Sangria.

SERVES ABOUT 6

Apple Kir

● 1 OZ (2 TBSP) THAWED	● 4 OZ (½ CUP) CLUB SODA
APPLE JUICE CONCENTRATE	● 1 THIN SLICE OF LEMON
● 1 TSP CRÈME DE CASSIS	ZEST
(BLACK CURRANT LIQUEUR)	

1 In a wine glass or Champagne flute, combine apple juice concentrate, crème de cassis, and club soda.

2 Garnish with lemon zest and serve immediately.

SERVES 1

The Coffee Bean

● 1½ OZ (3 TBSP) VODKA	● TWIST OF LEMON RIND
● 1½ OZ (3 TBSP) COFFEE	
LIQUEUR	

This is like the classic Black Russian, but uses more coffee liqueur. We feel it's a smoother, richer drink.

1 Shake vodka and liqueur together with ice.

2 Strain into ice-filled Old-fashioned glass. Top with lemon.

SERVES 1

Cranberry Cooler

● 1½ OZ (3 TBSP) WHITE	● ½ OZ (1 TBSP) LIME JUICE
RUM	● 1 TO 2 TSP SUGAR SYRUP
● ½ OZ (1 TBSP) CRANBERRY	(PAGE 13)
LIQUEUR	

This drink is for our friend Mary Ann Zimmerman, who loves cranberries.

1 Combine rum, cranberry liqueur, lime juice, and syrup in a shaker with plenty of ice.

2 Stir and strain over ice in Old-fashioned glass.

SERVES 1

Hot Buttered Rum

● 8 OZ (1 CUP) APPLE CIDER	● 2 OZ (4 TBSP) DARK
● 6 WHOLE CLOVES	JAMAICAN RUM
● 1 CINNAMON STICK	● 1 TSP BUTTER
● ½ OZ (1 TBSP) LEMON	
JUICE	

1 In a small saucepan, combine apple cider, cloves, cinnamon stick, and lemon juice and bring to a boil.

2 Pour mixture into a mug, add rum, top with butter, and serve immediately.

SERVES 1

Gin Fizz

• 3 OZ (6 TBSP) **TANQUERAY**	• 1 TBSP CONFECTIONERS
GIN	SUGAR
• 1½ OZ (3 TBSP) LEMON	• 2 TO 4 OZ (¼ TO ½ CUP)
JUICE	CLUB SODA
• 1 OZ (2 TBSP) LIME JUICE	• LIME WEDGE

1 Combine Tanqueray gin, lemon juice, lime juice, and sugar and stir until sugar is dissolved.

2 Pour drink into Tom Collins glass, top with club soda to fill glass, add ice, garnish with a lime wedge, and serve.

SERVES 1

Bitter Orange

• 2 OZ (¼ CUP) **TANQUERAY**	• 4 OZ (½ CUP) ORANGE
GIN	JUICE
	• DASH OF BITTERS

This is like a screwdriver but with slightly more liquor and slightly more bite.

1 Combine Tanqueray gin, orange juice, and bitters in a shaker with plenty of ice.

2 Shake well and strain into a Tom Collins glass with a couple of ice cubes.

SERVES 1

Tequila Manhattan

● 2 OZ (4 TBSP) TEQUILA	● 1½ OZ (3 TBSP) SWEET
	VERMOUTH

1 Combine tequila, vermouth, and ice in a glass. Stir for a few seconds to cool.

2 Pour drink into Old-fashioned glass, straining out ice if desired.

SERVES 1.

Vermouth Cassis

● 2 OZ (¼ CUP) DRY	● ¼ OZ (½ TBSP) CRÈME DE
VERMOUTH	CASSIS

We enjoy the simple version of this drink, just vermouth and crème de cassis. However, it's also nice as a tall, cool drink mixed with plenty of chilled club soda.

1 Pour vermouth and crème de cassis into a shaker with ice.

2 Stir and strain into Martini glass.

SERVES 1

Note

As an alternative, pour vermouth and crème de cassis into a Tom Collins glass filled with ice. Top the glass with club soda.

Collins

● 2½ OZ (5 TBSP)	● 2 TSP SUGAR SYRUP
TANQUERAY GIN	(PAGE 13)
● 2 OZ (4 TBSP) LEMON JUICE	● 2 TO 4 OZ (¼ TO ½ CUP)
● MINT	CLUB SODA

1 Combine Tanqueray gin, lemon juice, and sugar syrup. Stir until combined.

2 Pour drink into a Tom Collins glass, top with club soda to fill glass, add ice, garnish with fresh mint, and serve.

SERVES 1

Screwdriver

● 3 OZ (6 TBSP) FRESH	● 2 TSP LEMON JUICE
ORANGE JUICE	● ORANGE WEDGE
● 1 OZ (2 TBSP) **TANQUERAY**	

1 Combine orange juice, Tanqueray, and lemon juice in an Old-fashioned glass.

2 Add ice, garnish with an orange wedge, and serve.

SERVES 1

Mai Tai

● 2 OZ (4 TBSP) DARK RUM	● 1 TSP SUGAR SYRUP
● 1 OZ (2 TBSP) LIME JUICE	(PAGE 13)
● ⅓ OZ (2 TSP) COINTREAU	● WEDGE OF FRUIT
● ⅓ OZ (2 TSP) APRICOT	
BRANDY	

1 Combine dark rum, lime juice, Cointreau, apricot brandy, sugar syrup, and ice in an Old-fashioned glass.

2 Garnish with a wedge of fresh fruit.

SERVES 1

Black and White

● 1½ OZ (3 TBSP) DRY,	● TWIST OF LEMON RIND
WHITE VERMOUTH	
● 1½ OZ (3 TBSP) SWEET	
RED VERMOUTH	

Contrasts: Dry, white vermouth mixed with an equal amount of sweet, red vermouth makes a pleasant drink that's not too dry and not too sweet.

1 Combine both vermouths in an Old-fashioned glass.

2 Stir and add ice. Garnish with lemon rind.

SERVES 1

Champagne Cocktail

● ½ TSP SUGAR SYRUP	● 4 OUNCES (½ CUP)
(PAGE 13)	GOOD-QUALITY DRY
● DASH OF BITTERS	CHAMPAGNE, WELL CHILLED

1 Stir together syrup and bitters in a fluted Champagne glass. Don't get too generous with the bitters; you can correct the proportions by adding more to taste later.

2 Pour in the Champagne and stir once. Taste and add more bitters if desired.

SERVES 1

Black, White, and *Tanqueray* Gin All Over

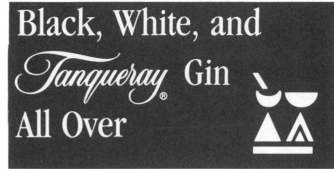

● 1 OZ (2 TBSP) DRY WHITE	● 1 OZ (2 TBSP) **TANQUERAY**
VERMOUTH	GIN
● 1 OZ (2 TBSP) SWEET RED	
VERMOUTH	

If you thought our Black and White drink was nice, perhaps you're ready for its tasteful cousin, made with the addition of Tanqueray gin.

1 Combine dry and sweet vermouths with Tanqueray gin in a shaker with ice.

2 Stir to chill. Strain into a Martini glass.

SERVES 1

Planter's Punch

● 2 OZ (¼ CUP) DARK RUM	● DASH OF GRENADINE
● 3 OZ (6 TBSP) ORANGE	● DASH OF BITTERS
JUICE	● MARASCHINO CHERRY
● ½ OZ (1 TBSP) LEMON	● ORANGE SLICE
JUICE	
● 1 TSP SUGAR SYRUP	
(PAGE 13)	

1 In a shaker with ice, combine rum, orange juice, lemon juice, sugar syrup, grenadine, and bitters. Shake well.

2 Strain mixture into an ice-filled Tom Collins glass. Garnish with cherry and orange slice.

SERVES 1

Pear Flip

● 1 OZ (2 TBSP) PEAR	● 1 EGG
LIQUEUR	● 2 TSP SUPERFINE SUGAR
● 1 OZ (2 TBSP) BRANDY	● CINNAMON STICK
● 1 TSP LEMON JUICE	(OPTIONAL)

Admittedly, this isn't everyone's cup of brew but those who like a little sustenance will flip for it.

1 Combine pear liqueur, brandy, lemon juice, egg, and sugar in a shaker with ice.

2 Shake well, then strain into a wine glass. If desired, garnish with cinnamon stick.

SERVES 1

Note

Some people like this drink really frothy. To make it lighter, combine the liqueur, brandy, lemon juice, egg, and sugar with 1 to 2 ice cubes, in a blender and blend at high speed for 1 minute.

Rum Ricky

● 1½ OZ (3 TBSP) WHITE	● CLUB SODA, WELL CHILLED
RUM	● LIME WEDGE
● ½ OZ (1 TBSP) LIME JUICE	

If the temperature rises to 98 degrees on the day of your party, make this the official drink.

1 Combine rum and lime juice in an ice-filled shaker. Stir and strain into an ice-filled Tom Collins glass.

2 Fill with club soda and garnish with lime wedge.

SERVES 1

Note

A Ricky usually isn't sweet, but some people might find this drink too tart. If you like, stir in 1 teaspoon Sugar Syrup (page 13) with the rum and lime juice.

Tanqueray® Negroni

● ¾ OZ (1½ TBSP)	● ¾ OZ (1½ TBSP) SWEET
TANQUERAY GIN	RED VERMOUTH
● ¾ OZ (1½ TBSP) CAMPARI	● ORANGE SLICE

A classic drink with a slight bitter taste that many people have a taste for.

1 Combine Tanqueray gin, Campari, and vermouth in an ice-filled shaker.

2 Stir well and strain into a Martini glass. Garnish with an orange slice.

SERVES 1

Bittersweet Sherry

Rummy Sherry

● 1½ OZ (3 TBSP) DRY	● ¼ OZ (½ TBSP) CAMPARI
SHERRY	
● ½ OZ (1 TBSP) SWEET RED	
VERMOUTH	

1 Combine dry sherry, sweet vermouth, and Campari in a shaker with ice.

2 Stir and strain into a Martini glass.

SERVES 1

● 2 OZ (¼ CUP) WHITE RUM	● ORANGE SLICE
● 1 OZ (2 TBSP) DRY SHERRY	

The combination of rum and sherry is light and dry—quite good.

1 Combine rum and sherry in a shaker with ice.

2 Stir and strain into an ice-filled Old-fashioned glass. Garnish with orange slice.

SERVES 1

Orange Whiskey

Berry Brandy

● 2 OZ (¼ CUP) WHISKEY	● 1 TSP SUPERFINE SUGAR
● 1 OZ (2 TBSP) GRAND	(OPTIONAL)
MARNIER	● ORANGE SLICE
● ½ OZ (1 TBSP) LEMON	
JUICE	

1 Combine whiskey, Grand Marnier, lemon juice, and sugar, if used, in a shaker with ice.

2 Stir and strain into an Old-fashioned glass filled with 1 or 2 ice cubes. Garnish with orange slice.

SERVES 1

● 1½ OZ (3 TBSP) BRANDY	● 2 OZ (¼ CUP) CLUB SODA,
● ½ OZ (1 TBSP) FRAISE DES	WELL CHILLED (OPTIONAL)
BOIS LIQUEUR	
● ½ OZ (1 TBSP) LEMON	
JUICE	

This tart brandy drink is fine plain or with a splash of soda.

1 Combine brandy, fraise des bois liqueur, and lemon juice in ice-filled shaker.

2 Stir and strain into Old-fashioned glass. Add 1 or 2 ice cubes. Add club soda if desired.

SERVES 1

Opposite: Steamed Broccoli with Gorgonzola Mayonnaise (recipe on page 55); and Red Sangria (recipe on page 20). Following pages: Asparagus in the Pink (recipe on page 56); and Whiskey Sour (recipe on page 25). Mint Julep (recipe on page 26). Liptauer with Lettuce Flower (recipe on page 57).

SPECTACULARS

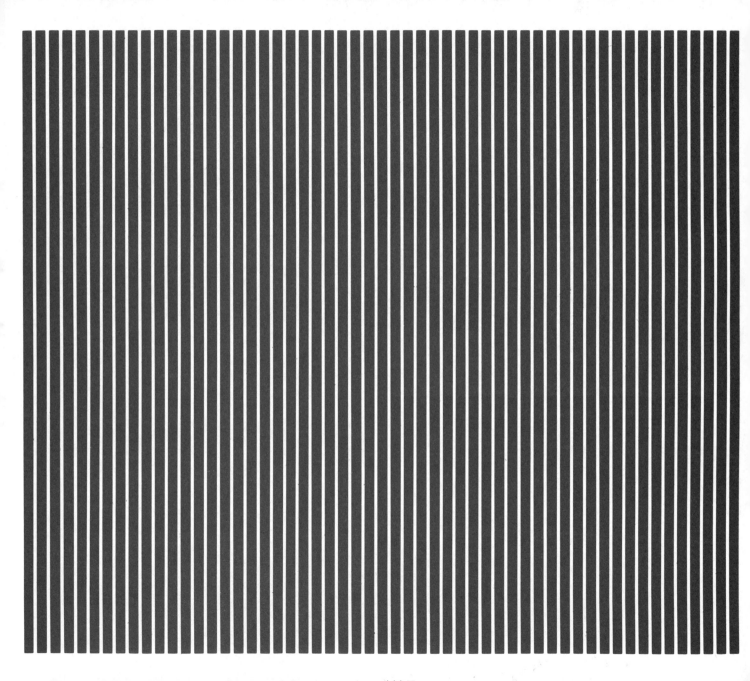

The word says it.

These are the dishes that tell guests they're special.

Arrange asparagus spears in a vase filled with salmon pink mayonnaise. It's a delightful spring bouquet.

Light a dim evening with Saganaki, the flaming cheese dish from Greece.

Make a show of sumptuousness by offering crêpes filled and topped with caviar.

Decorate a table with a whimsical flower of lettuce rooted in liptaur cheese.

. . . And, don't let anyone know how easy these dishes are.

Layered Torte in a Hollowed-Out Bread

• 2 CLOVES GARLIC, PEELED	• FRESHLY GROUND BLACK
AND MINCED	PEPPER
• 4 TBSP BUTTER	• 1 RED BELL PEPPER
• ½ TSP GROUND NUTMEG	• 1 ROUND LOAF ITALIAN
• 2 PACKAGES (10 OZ EACH)	BREAD (6½ IN. DIAMETER)
FROZEN, CHOPPED	• 8 OZ SWISS CHEESE, SLICED
SPINACH, DEFROSTED AND	• 4 OZ PEPPERONI, THINLY
SQUEEZED DRY	SLICED
• ½ CUP PLUS 2 TBSP	• OLIVE OIL
GRATED PARMESAN CHEESE	

1 Preheat oven to 350 degrees. Over very low heat, sauté garlic in 2 tablespoons butter for 1 minute. Do not allow garlic or butter to brown. Add nutmeg and sauté, stirring constantly, for 30 seconds more.

2 Separate spinach and add to sauté pan along with remaining 2 tablespoons of butter and Parmesan cheese. Sauté until cheese is melted. Cool. Season to taste with pepper.

3 Core pepper and slice in pieces 1 inch by ½ inch. Simmer in water until pepper is soft. Drain and pat dry with paper towel.

4 Cut top 1½ inches from bread. Remove all but a ¼-inch layer of bread from inside crust. (Leftover bread can be used to make bread crumbs.) Line bottom and sides of bread cavity with some slices of Swiss cheese. Divide remaining cheese into 3 parts.

5 Spread bottom with half the spinach mixture, smoothing into an even layer. Place a layer of cheese on top. Pat oil off of pepperoni with a paper towel, and arrange half the pepperoni over cheese. Sprinkle peppers over and top with remaining pepperoni slices. Place layer of cheese on top. Spread remaining spinach over and top with remaining cheese.

6 Place top of bread on loaf and brush entire bread liberally with olive oil. Wrap tightly with foil and bake for 25 minutes, or until cheese on top begins to melt. Refrigerate until torte is thoroughly cooled. Serve cold or tepid.

SERVES 6 TO 8

47

Saganaki (Flaming Greek Cheese)

● OLIVE OIL FOR	● 1 EGG, LIGHTLY BEATEN
DEEP-FRYING	● 1 OZ (2 TBSP) BRANDY OR
● ¼ CUP ALL-PURPOSE FLOUR	COGNAC
● SALT AND FRESHLY GROUND	● JUICE OF ½ LEMON
BLACK PEPPER	● CRUSTY FRENCH OR ITALIAN
● 1 PIECE (6 OZ) KASSERI	BREAD
CHEESE, ABOUT ¾ IN.	
THICK, 6 BY 4 IN. WIDE	

Greek kasseri cheese set aflame is a dramatic way to warm up any party. You'll find kasseri cheese in Greek food stores and in supermarkets that specialize in international foods.

1 Preheat ½ inch of olive oil to 350 degrees in a frying pan. Season flour to taste with salt and pepper, then dip cheese in egg and in flour. Gently slide cheese into hot oil and fry on one side for 2 minutes or until golden. Turn cheese over and fry for an additional 1 minute on the other side, or until it is golden.

2 With a slotted spatula, remove cheese from oil and place on a flameproof platter. Pour brandy or Cognac over and ignite with a kitchen match. Allow to burn for a few seconds and then douse flame with the juice of ½ lemon. (Keep a saucepan lid handy to place over the flaming cheese in the event that the lemon juice does not put out the flame.) Serve immediately with pieces of bread to absorb the lemon and brandy on the platter.

SERVES 2 TO 4

Tandoori Kabobs

● 4 CHICKEN BREAST HALVES	● 1 TSP GOOD-QUALITY
● 3 TBSP LEMON JUICE	PAPRIKA
● 3 LARGE CLOVES GARLIC,	● ½ CUP PLAIN YOGURT
MINCED FINE	● 3 LEMONS, EACH CUT
● 1 TBSP MINCED	VERTICALLY INTO 6 WEDGES
GINGERROOT	**ONION RELISH**
● 1 TSP CRUSHED CUMIN	● 1 LB ONIONS
SEED	● SALT AND WHITE PEPPER
● ¼ TSP GROUND CARDAMOM	TO TASTE
● ¼ TSP GROUND CLOVES	● 1 TBSP MINCED FRESH
● ¼ TO ½ TSP CRUSHED RED	CORIANDER (CILANTRO)
PEPPER FLAKES	

Beer or Black Velvet, that frothy blend of stout and Champagne, will stand up to this highly seasoned chicken dish.

1 Skin and bone raw chicken. Cut meat into 1-inch squares. Toss with lemon juice and set aside in glass bowl for 30 minutes.

2 Meanwhile combine garlic, ginger, cumin seed, cardamom, cloves, red pepper, paprika, and yogurt. Stir well and spoon into chicken mixture. Set aside at room temperature up to 2 hours or 4 hours refrigerated. While chicken is marinating soak 16 to 18 wooden skewers in cold water.

3 Preheat oven to 500 degrees. Thread 2 chicken cubes (or 3 smaller ones) on each skewer. Place skewers on rack that is set on a cookie sheet or shallow roasting pan. Roast for 10 minutes or until chicken is done.

4 Prepare onion relish. Peel and slice onions as thinly as possible. Separate into rings. Soak in cold water for 15 minutes. Gently press out water. Sprinkle with salt and pepper to taste and toss with coriander.

5 Make a bed of onion relish on serving platter. Top with Tandoori Kabobs and garnish with lemon wedges. Chicken can be served warm or at room temperature.

SERVES 16 TO 18

Cheese Terrine with Pinenuts and Strawberries

Although this recipe looks long, it's very easy to make, and the presentation is beautiful and elegant. It's one of our favorites.

1 Butter a 5-cup loaf terrine and line it with waxed paper. Remove crust from brie and whip brie in food processor, blender, or with hand mixer until cheese is fluffy. Set aside. Discard crust.

2 Combine blue cheese and pinenuts and whip until cheese is fluffy.

3 Divide brie into thirds. Spread one portion of brie in an even layer on the bottom of the terrine. Refrigerate for 30 minutes.

4 Spread half of the blue cheese/pinenut mixture in an even layer over the top of the brie. Refrigerate for 30 minutes.

5 Continue layering (brie, blue cheese, brie), refrigerating 30 minutes after each layering. End with brie. Cover tightly and refrigerate overnight.

6 To unmold, gently ease knife around edges between paper and terrine, being careful not to rip paper.

7 Lower terrine into very warm water almost up to the top of the terrine. Count to 10. Remove from water, dry terrine, cover with serving dish, and quickly invert terrine and dish. If loaf does not drop out onto dish, repeat water dunking. It probably will take several such water baths for cheese to melt enough around the edges so that it drops out of the terrine.

● 2 LB SOFTENED BRIE CHEESE	● ½ PINT STRAWBERRIES
	● MINT LEAVES
● 7 OZ BLUE CHEESE	● NORWEGIAN FLAT BREAD
● 4 TBSP PINENUTS (PIGNOLI), GROUND	

50

8 When unmolded, peel off paper and smooth the surface with a knife.

9 Clean and dry strawberries. Slice lengthwise and, by overlapping, decorate top of cheese.

10 Garnish with a few mint leaves at the bottom center of each of the long sides. Serve cold or tepid with Norwegian flat bread.

SERVES 12 TO 14

Note
Cheese Terrine with Pinenuts and Strawberries can be made several days in advance, covered with plastic wrap, and refrigerated until serving.

An Appetizer Cheesecake

● 60 WHEAT CRACKERS, EACH	● 1 TBSP GRATED ONION
1-IN. SQUARE	PULP OR PURÉE
● 2 TBSP BUTTER, MELTED	● DASH OF LEMON JUICE
● 2 LB CREAM CHEESE, AT	● ¼ TSP FRESHLY GRATED
ROOM TEMPERATURE	BLACK PEPPER
● 4 EGGS, AT ROOM	● 1 CUP GROUND PECANS
TEMPERATURE	● 1 LARGE OR 2 SMALL
● 8 OZ STILTON CHEESE	CLOVES GARLIC
● 2 PACKED CUPS	● ¼ TSP SALT
WATERCRESS LEAVES,	● PECAN HALVES
WASHED AND DRIED	

People who know us know that we'll use any excuse to make a cheesecake, even a cocktail party. Like all cheesecakes, this one is very rich and should be served in small portions. It is inspired by Maida Heatter.

1 Finely crush the crackers by hand or in a food processor. Toss with melted butter and press onto bottom and ½ inch up the sides of a 9-inch spring-form pan. Chill in refrigerator.

2 Beat cream cheese in an electric mixer until light and fluffy. Add eggs, one at a time, beating each in before adding the next. Scrape rind off stilton cheese and discard. Crumble cheese.

3 Pour 1 cup cream cheese batter into a second bowl. Mix in stilton, beating well until mixture is fairly smooth with only small crumbs of stilton noticeable. Spread stilton mixture gently over crust. Smooth mixture with a wet spoon, if necessary. Place in freezer for 1 hour.

4 Meanwhile, finely mince watercress. Reserve half. Combine remaining minced watercress with 2 cups cream cheese, onion pulp, lemon juice, and pepper. If a strong, green-colored layer is desired, process the mixture in a blender or food processor for a minute. (This looks very attractive; if this step is omitted, the watercress mixture will be cream-colored with green flecks.)

5 Combine ground pecans with remaining cream cheese. Peel garlic. Mash with salt to make a paste, then stir into nut mixture, combining thoroughly.

6 Remove cheesecake from freezer. Sprinkle with reserved minced watercress. Gently pour watercress-cheese mixture over stilton layer. Return to the freezer for 30 minutes.

7 Preheat oven to 325 degrees. Remove cheesecake from freezer. Gently spread with nut mixture. Place cheesecake inside larger pan, about 4 inches deep. Fill pan with enough hot water to come halfway up the springform pan. Place pan in oven and bake for 45 minutes.

8 Remove from oven and arrange pecan halves around the edge of the cake. Return to oven for another 45 minutes or until cake feels firm and looks faintly browned.

9 Remove cake from oven and allow to cool completely at room temperature. Chill several hours before serving.

SERVES 20

Buckwheat Crêpes with Caviar

• 1 EGG, AT ROOM TEMPERATURE	• ¼ CUP ALL-PURPOSE FLOUR
• 1 EGG YOLK, AT ROOM TEMPERATURE	• 1 TBSP BUTTER, MELTED
• 1¼ CUPS MILK	• 2 TBSP CLARIFIED BUTTER
• ½ TSP SUGAR	• 1¼ CUPS SOUR CREAM
• DASH OF SALT	• 2 JARS (2 OZ EACH) CAVIAR, EITHER RED SALMON OR GOLDEN WHITEFISH
• ½ CUP BUCKWHEAT FLOUR	• MINT LEAVES (OPTIONAL)

1 In a bowl, beat together egg, egg yolk, and 1 cup milk. Combine sugar, salt, buckwheat flour, and all-purpose flour and stir. Whisk into egg mixture. Stir in melted butter and set batter aside at room temperature for 30 minutes.

2 Stir batter before using. It has a tendency to get thick, so stir in up to ¼ cup more milk to make a batter the consistency of thin pancake batter.

3 Brush a 5-inch, heavy-bottomed skillet with clarified butter and place over medium-low heat. Add ½ tablespoon batter and rotate skillet (it may be necessary to encourage this relatively elastic batter with a spoon) to make a 3-inch crêpe. Cook for 1 to 1½ minutes on one side; turn over and cook about 30 seconds on the second side. Slide crêpe out onto plate and repeat with remaining batter, brushing pan with clarified butter as needed.

4 To assemble, spread about 1 teaspoon sour cream on each crêpe. Top with ½ teaspoon caviar and roll up. Place seam-side down on serving dish. Top each crêpe roll with an additional ½ teaspoon sour cream and dot with more caviar. Garnish with a mint sprig if desired. Chill 1 to 2 hours, then serve.

SERVES 16

Note

Plain crêpes freeze very well. Place a sheet of plastic wrap between crêpes, then wrap the entire stack in heavy-duty foil.

54

Steamed Broccoli with Gorgonzola Mayonnaise

● 1 CUP CRUMBLED GORGONZOLA CHEESE	● 1 LARGE EGG YOLK, AT ROOM TEMPERATURE
● 1 TBSP VEGETABLE OIL	● ¼ TSP SALT
● 1 TBSP LEMON JUICE	● 14 OZ LIGHTLY STEAMED BROCCOLI FLOWERETS
● 1 WHOLE LARGE EGG, AT ROOM TEMPERATURE	

This dish is perfect as an impressive, last-minute snack. In fact, it is meant to be made just before serving since the sauce hardens when refrigerated.

1 In a blender or food processor, whirl cheese, oil, and lemon juice together until a paste is made. Add egg, egg yolk, and salt and blend until fluffy, about 1 minute.

2 Pour Gorgonzola Mayonnaise onto serving plate. Arrange broccoli in the center to form a circular mound. Serve immediately.

SERVES 6 TO 8 (MAKES ⅔ CUP MAYONNAISE)

Note
Cheese should be primarily white. Highly veined gorgonzola will ruin the golden color of this rich mayonnaise.

Asparagus in the Pink

Skip the flowers. For a smashing centerpiece for a Spring party, arrange fresh asparagus in a pool of pink mayonnaise. This looks equally lovely if artichokes are used.

● 1½ JARS (4 OZ EACH)	● 6 TBSP VEGETABLE OIL
PIMIENTOS	● 6 TBSP OLIVE OIL
● 1 TBSP TOMATO PASTE	● SALT AND WHITE PEPPER
● 1 EGG, AT ROOM	● DASH OF LEMON JUICE
TEMPERATURE	● 2 TO 3 LB ASPARAGUS
● 1 EGG YOLK, AT ROOM	
TEMPERATURE	

1 Drain pimientos. Pat dry on paper towels. Place in blender and turn on to finely mince. Add tomato paste, egg, and egg yolk. Stir together the 2 oils, then pour ¼ cup of the oil mixture into the egg mixture. Turn machine on for 30 seconds to mix ingredients together.

2 With machine running (at blend speed), drizzle in remaining oil. Scrape bowl of blender down into mixture. Season with salt and pepper to taste, and lemon juice. Pour mayonnaise into glass pitchers or glass vases and refrigerate while cooking asparagus.

3 Break tough parts of stalks off asparagus. Steam asparagus 8 minutes or until tender. Cool and pat dry. Arrange asparagus in pitchers with mayonnaise as if it were a flower arrangement. Allow guests to pluck out asparagus with its mayonnaise dip.

SERVES ABOUT 10 TO 15 (MAKES ABOUT 1⅓ CUPS MAYONNAISE)

Note

Both the asparagus and the mayonnaise can be made a day in advance, well wrapped and stored in the refrigerator. Put together just before serving.

Liptaur with a Lettuce Flower

One of the prettiest selections in this book, Liptaur with a Lettuce Flower takes only minutes to prepare (although it requires refrigeration) and can be used as a natural centerpiece. Liptaur also is excellent served as a spread with toasted Bagel Thins (page 67).

1 With an electric mixer, blender, or food processor, whip together cream cheese, butter, yogurt, marjoram, paprika, salt, capers, and chives. Refrigerate until firm.

2 Wash lettuce or radicchio and dry well. Trim off bottom 2 inches. Pack liptaur into a bowl with a 2½-cup capacity. Stick greens in cheese to make a flower design. Serve cold. Each lettuce leaf will have a small amount of cheese on it.

SERVES 6 TO 8 (MAKES ABOUT 2 CUPS)

• 11 OZ CREAM CHEESE, SOFTENED	• ¼ TSP SALT
• 4 TBSP BUTTER, SOFTENED	• 1 HEAPING TBSP CAPERS
• 1 TBSP PLAIN YOGURT	• ½ CUP FRESH CHIVES, MINCED
• ½ TSP DRIED MARJORAM	• 1 HEAD OF RED-LEAF LETTUCE OR RADICCHIO
• 1½ TSP PAPRIKA	

Scallops in Pea-Pod Beds

● 4 OZ PEA PODS	● ¼ CUP HEAVY CREAM
● 1 CUP DRY WHITE WINE	● FRESH CORIANDER LEAVES
● FRESH DILL SPRIGS	(CILANTRO)
● 8 OZ BAY SCALLOPS	● LEMON WEDGES
● 1⅓ CUPS HERBED CHEESE	
(PAGE 196)	

1 Steam pea pods for 3 to 5 minutes. Set aside to cool. Pat dry.

2 Place wine in a nonaluminum saucepan with 1 or 2 dill sprigs. Bring to a boil, then add bay scallops. Cover. Reduce heat to medium. Count to 60, then remove scallops from heat. Strain off liquid and dill and discard. Pat scallops dry and allow to cool.

3 Cream together herbed cheese and cream. Stem pea pods and form opening in tops. Using a knife tip or pastry tube, fill each pea pod with ½ to 1½ teaspoons cheese mixture. The amount will vary with the size of the pod.

4 Fit in 2 or 3 scallops on top of the cheese to resemble peas. Garnish each pea pod with a coriander leaf. Arrange stuffed pea pods on coriander-lined platter. Decorate with lemon wedges.

SERVES 20

Note
Chill several hours before serving, but don't make more than 8 hours in advance.

Opposite: Scallops in Snow-pea Pods; and Gimlet (recipe on page 24). Following pages: Baked Garlic (recipe on page 64). Macademia Nut Chicken Pieces (recipe on page 66). Rainbow Vegetable Terrine (recipe on page 68).

NOT HALF-BAKED

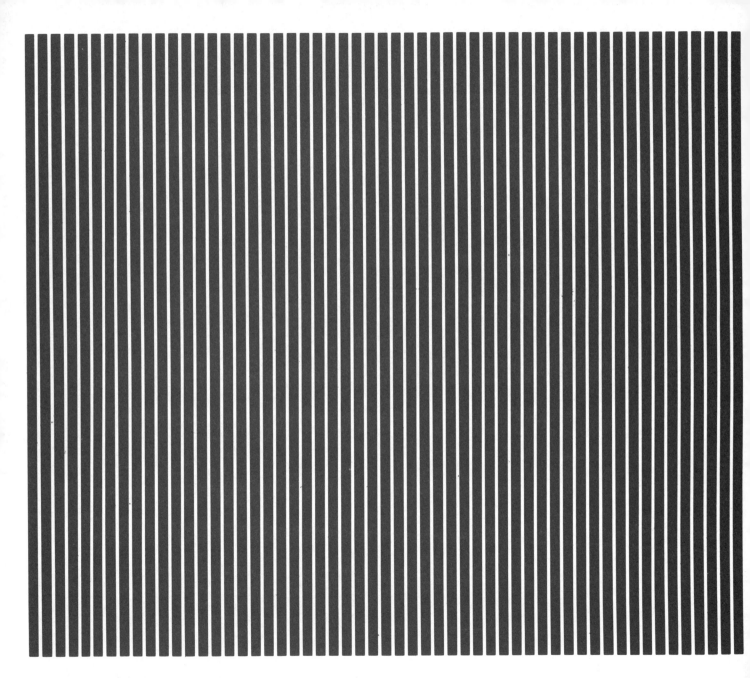

A collection of baked foods—from a simple Gingered Sausage to an elaborate Rainbow Vegetable Terrine with Cognac—is the foundation for a party menu.

There's the familiar Roast Beef, dressed up with a sharp Horseradish Cream, Cold Turkey with a ribbon of ham and cheese in the center, and Skewered Snails Wrapped in Bacon.

Or surprise your guests. Hide baked garlic in a bread case and allow them to discover the creamy, mild-tasting spread it can be.

Zucchini Cups

● 3 LARGE ZUCCHINI (ABOUT	● 1 CUP FINELY CRUMBLED
1½ LB), TRIMMED	FETA CHEESE
● ½ CUP GRATED GRUYÈRE	● 2 EGGS, BEATEN
CHEESE	● FRESHLY GROUND WHITE
● 1 HEAPING TBSP MINCED	PEPPER
FRESH BASIL	● CUCUMBER CURLS

1 Preheat oven to 350 degrees. Wash zucchini. Cut into 1-inch-thick slices. Using a melon scoop, scoop out a hole on one cut side of zucchini, leaving cup with a ¼-inch-thick wall. Combine gruyère cheese, basil, feta, eggs, and pepper. Spoon filling into zucchini cups allowing ½ to 1½ tablespoons filling per cup, depending on size of cavity.

2 Place zucchini on cookie sheet. Bake for 30 minutes, until cheese is hot and puffed up. Place on serving platter and garnish with cucumber curls. Serve warm or tepid.

SERVES 10

Baked Garlic

● 3 HEADS (THESE ARE	● SALT AND WHITE PEPPER
HEADS, NOT CLOVES)	● 1 ROUND ITALIAN BREAD,
GARLIC	ABOUT 1½ LB
● 2 TBSP CLARIFIED BUTTER	● 4 TBSP BUTTER, MELTED
● 2 TBSP CHICKEN BROTH	
● 3 SPRIGS (1½ TO 2 INCHES	
EACH) FRESH ROSEMARY,	
OR ½ TEASPOON DRIED	
ROSEMARY	

It might take a bit of coaxing to convince guests that this garlic appetizer won't put a crimp in their socializing. Baked garlic is sweet and inoffensive, and, we might add, very sensuous.

1 Preheat oven to 300 degrees. Remove outer paper skin from garlic heads. Don't separate into cloves. Fit heads into a 1¾-cup ovenproof dish.

2 Combine butter and chicken broth and pour over garlic. Arrange rosemary around garlic (or sprinkle with dried rosemary). Season with salt and pepper to taste. Bake for 1 hour, 15 minutes, basting every 15 minutes with butter mixture.

3 Meanwhile, cut a 3- to 4-inch circle off the top of the bread and reserve the top. Hollow out the inside, leaving a ½-inch shell. (Bread can be frozen and used for bread crumbs or bread pudding.) Cut bread in half, starting from the top, leaving about 1 to 2 inches joined at the bottom. Then cut each half into 4 wedges, leaving bottom joined. Place sheet of foil on cookie sheet. Place bread on top of it.

4 Brush inside of bread and inside of bread top with melted butter. Place in oven during last 15 minutes garlic is baking and warm through.

5 To serve, place bread in an attractive bowl (a round straw basket is wonderful) and arrange garlic heads inside. Cover with bread lid. Allow guests to remove bread lid, take off a garlic clove and pinch it to remove the skin. Then guests can tear off part of the bread and spread the softened garlic on it.

SERVES 8

Roast Beef with Horseradish Cream

	HORSERADISH CREAM
● 1 TOP ROUND ROAST,	
ABOUT 4 TO 5 LB (SEE	● 1 CUP HEAVY CREAM
NOTE)	● ¼ CUP WELL-DRAINED
	WHITE HORSERADISH
	● 2 TBSP PREPARED
	MUSTARD

Carnivores supposedly are a dying breed. Don't believe it. Put this platter of roast beef with horseradish cream on the table and watch it disappear.

1 Preheat oven to 325 degrees. Place roast on rack in shallow roasting pan that has been lined with foil. Place in oven and allow 25 minutes per pound (25 minutes yields a medium-rare roast; 30 minutes will yield a roast that's fairly well done with a little pink in the center). If using a meat thermometer, it should indicate 130 to 135 degrees for medium doneness.

2 Remove meat from oven (cut off strings and fat; see note). Allow to come to room temperature, then chill.

3 Prepare Horseradish Cream. Whip cream until stiff. Fold in horseradish and mustard. This makes about 2 cups cream. The cream will hold up several hours if wrapped with plastic wrap and stored in the refrigerator.

4 When ready to serve, slice meat as thinly as possible and arrange on serving platter with horseradish cream in the center. Estimate 1 or 2 slices of meat per person if including a full array of other foods.

SERVES 30 TO 40

Note

If butcher doesn't do it automatically, ask for a thin layer of fat to be wrapped around the roast and tied at 1- to 2-inch intervals. Make sure butcher keeps roast as evenly shaped as possible.

Macadamia Nut Chicken Pieces

● 2 CUPS ALL-PURPOSE FLOUR	● 1 LB BONED CHICKEN
● SALT (1 TO 2 TSP,	BREAST, CUT IN STRIPS ¾
DEPENDING UPON	IN. WIDE AND 3 IN. LONG
SALTINESS OF THE NUTS)	● ½ CUP BUTTER, MELTED
● 12 OZ ROASTED	● 4 EGGS, LIGHTLY BEATEN
MACADAMIA NUTS, FINELY	
CHOPPED	

This is one of our favorite cocktail foods. Whoever makes it will have messy hands, but will get to sample the nutty, buttery chicken as it comes from the oven. Serve Macadamia Nut Chicken Pieces solo or with the Honey Mustard outlined in Garlic Sausage in Pastry (page 95).

1 Preheat oven to 350 degrees. Pour flour mixed with salt into a plastic bag. Pour macadamia nuts into another plastic bag.

2 With a small handful at a time, dip chicken strips in melted butter to coat. Place in flour-filled bag and shake to coat. Shake excess flour off chicken and dip in egg. Shake off excess egg and place in macadamia nut-filled plastic bag. Shake to coat.

3 Place chicken strips on ungreased, nonstick cookie sheet. Repeat with remaining chicken pieces. Bake 20 minutes. Store in refrigerator in an airtight container, then serve tepid.

SERVES 20

Note

Macadamia Nut Chicken Pieces are best if made the day they are to be served.

Broiled Garlic Bagel Thins

• 5 COMMERCIALLY PREPARED BAGELS	• 6 CLOVES GARLIC, MINCED
	• 2 TBSP LEMON JUICE
• ½ CUP BUTTER	• SALT (OPTIONAL)

If the almost overpowering scent of garlic does not fit your mood, try these Bagel Thins sliced and browned, dry, in the toaster. They make a perfect accompaniment for Hummus in Red Pepper Shells (page 150).

1 Preheat broiler. Slice bagels crosswise into fifths. Melt butter with garlic and simmer over very low heat for about 2 minutes or until garlic is softened. Add lemon juice and salt to taste. Liberally brush 1 side of each bagel slice with lemon-garlic butter.

2 Broil bagels on one side until golden. Watch carefully; this only takes a minute. Turn bagels over and broil on the other side until golden. Serve hot or tepid.

SERVES 10 TO 12 (25 BAGEL THINS)

Note
Broiled Garlic Bagel Thins can be made a day in advance and stored in an airtight container.

Rainbow Vegetable Terrine with Cognac

This rainbow of vegetables doesn't rely on fancy spices for its flavors but takes character from butter, cream, and Cognac as they play to the vegetables.

1 Set julienned carrots aside to be used as garnish. Sauté remaining carrots in butter over very low heat until carrots are tender. Do not allow carrots or butter to brown. Cool. Remove carrots from butter with a slotted spoon. Purée in blender or food processor until smooth. Add nutmeg, allspice, sugar, heavy cream, Cognac, egg, and egg yolk and blend. Set aside.

2 Simmer broccoli in water until broccoli is tender. Cool. In a blender or food processor, purée broccoli (except pieces being used for garnish) with heavy cream, butter, nutmeg, salt, and egg. Set aside purée and broccoli pieces.

3 Sauté potato and onion in butter until potato pieces are tender and onion is soft. Do not allow potatoes, onion, or butter to brown. Cool. Purée potatoes, onion, and butter in blender or food processor with heavy cream, Cognac, curry powder, salt, white pepper to taste, egg, and egg yolk. Set aside.

4 Preheat oven to 350 degrees. Butter a 5-cup loaf terrine and line it with waxed paper. Cut another piece of waxed paper to fit the top of the terrine. Butter one side of the paper.

5 Pour carrot purée into bottom of the terrine. Smooth to make an even layer. Top with broccoli purée. Smooth to make an even layer. Top with potato purée and smooth to make an even layer.

CARROT LAYER	2 TBSP BUTTER
1½ CUPS SLICED CARROTS,	½ TSP GROUND NUTMEG
PLUS 4 JULIENNED PIECES	¼ TSP SALT
ABOUT ¼ IN. BY 2 IN.	1 EGG
2 TBSP BUTTER	POTATO LAYER
¾ TSP GROUND NUTMEG	1½ CUPS POTATO CHUNKS
⅛ TSP GROUND ALLSPICE	WITHOUT PEEL
½ TSP SUGAR	1 CUP CHOPPED ONION
2 TBSP HEAVY CREAM	4 TBSP BUTTER
1 TBSP COGNAC	¼ CUP HEAVY CREAM
1 EGG	1 TBSP COGNAC
1 EGG YOLK	1 TSP CURRY POWDER
BROCCOLI LAYER	¼ TSP SALT
2 CUPS FRESH BROCCOLI	WHITE PEPPER
PIECES, PLUS FOR GARNISH	1 EGG
2 TBSP HEAVY CREAM	1 EGG YOLK

Press waxed paper, butter side down, over potato purée. Place terrine in a pan and add enough hot water to come halfway up the outside of the terrine. Carefully place pan in oven, and bake for 1½ hours or until a knife inserted into center of loaf comes out clean. Turn off oven and open door. Allow terrine to rest for 15 minutes. Remove from oven to countertop.

6 When terrine is cool enough to handle, remove and discard waxed paper from top. Cover terrine with serving dish and quickly invert terrine and dish. Remove remaining waxed paper.

7 Garnish top of loaf by alternating remaining broccoli flowerets and carrots pieces in a sunburst design in the center, along one of the long sides. Refrigerate until chilled. Serve cold.

SERVES 8 TO 10

Baked Cashew Casserole

● 4 SCALLIONS, BOTH GREEN AND WHITE PARTS MINCED	● 1 EGG, LIGHTLY BEATEN
	● ½ CUP CHOPPED CASHEWS
● 3 TBSP BUTTER	● ¼ CUP MINCED FRESH PARSLEY
● ¾ CUP RICOTTA CHEESE	
● ½ CUP GRATED PARMESAN CHEESE	● 1 TOMATO ROSE
	● PUMPERNICKEL BREAD
● 4 OZ CREAM CHEESE	
● ¼ CUP LEMON JUICE	

1 Preheat oven to 375 degrees. Sauté scallions in butter until scallions are soft. In a blender, food processor, or with an electric mixer, cream together ricotta, Parmesan, cream cheese, lemon juice, and egg. Fold in scallions and cashews.

2 Pour mixture into a greased 2½-cup ovenproof dish. Cover top of cheese mixture with greased waxed paper, butter side down. Bake for 20 minutes or until casserole is hot.

3 Remove casserole from oven, take off the waxed paper, sprinkle casserole with parsley, and place a tomato rose in the center. Serve hot with sliced pumpernickel bread.

SERVES 6 TO 8

Note

To make a tomato rose, with a very sharp knife carefully remove the peel from 1 small tomato. Wind the peel around your finger to make a rose shape. It will maintain its shape when pressed into the top of the casserole.

Baked Feta Cheese

● 12 OZ FETA CHEESE	● 3 TBSP MINCED FRESH DILL
● 1¼ CUPS OLIVE OIL	● 1 CUP BREAD CRUMBS
● 2 LARGE CLOVES GARLIC,	● MANGO CHUTNEY
MINCED	(PAGE 191)

Serve Baked Feta Cheese solo or sprinkle it on a salad. It's salty, rich, and creamy when served hot.

1 Cut cheese into 24 cubes. Place cheese in a bowl with olive oil. Sprinkle with garlic and dill and allow to marinate, stirring occasionally, for at least 1 hour.

2 Preheat oven to 450 degrees. Remove cheese from oil, coat with bread crumbs, and place on an ungreased cookie sheet. Bake for 10 minutes or until cheese begins to turn golden. Serve hot or warm with Mango Chutney.

SERVES 10 TO 12

Skewered Snails Wrapped in Bacon

● 1 CAN (7 OZ) SNAILS	● FRESHLY GROUND BLACK
● 1 CUP DRY WHITE WINE	PEPPER
● 3 CLOVES GARLIC, MINCED	● 7 SLICES BACON
● 1 TBSP MINCED FRESH	(APPROXIMATELY)
PARSLEY	● SLICED RYE BREAD
● 1 BAY LEAF	● GARLIC-PARSLEY BUTTER
● JUICE OF ½ LEMON	(PAGE 189)

This will make a snail lover of even those who have never dared to sample them. First the snails are lightly seasoned with white wine, garlic, bay leaf, and lemon. Then they are grilled with bacon. The result is an almost sweet/smokey flavor.

1 Drain snails and rinse in cold water. In a saucepan, combine wine, garlic, parsley, bay leaf, lemon juice, and freshly ground black pepper to taste. Bring to a boil, remove from heat, and add snails. Marinate in the refrigerator for several hours or overnight. While snails are marinating, soak 7 to 10 bamboo skewers in cold water for at least 1 hour.

2 Cut bacon slices in thirds and use 1 piece to wrap around each snail. Thread onto a skewer. Repeat with remaining snails and bacon, using 2 or 3 snails per skewer. Broil (either over hot coals or in stove broiler) for a few minutes or until bacon is cooked. Serve hot with sliced rye bread and garlic butter.

SERVES 3 OR 4

Note

To prevent tips of bamboo skewers from turning color during broiling, cover them with foil.

Grilled Sesame Sirloin with White Radish Salad

	WHITE RADISH SALAD
• 1 TBSP SESAME SEEDS	
• 1 TBSP SESAME OIL	• 1½ CUPS SHREDDED WHITE
• 1 TSP MINCED GINGERROOT	RADISH
• 1 GARLIC CLOVE, MINCED	• 1 CARROT, SHREDDED
• 1 SCALLION, BOTH WHITE	• 1 TBSP LEMON JUICE
AND GREEN PARTS MINCED	• 2 TBSP SOY SAUCE
• 1 TO 2 TBSP HONEY	• 1 TSP SESAME OIL
• ¾ CUP SOY SAUCE	• 2 TBSP WHITE RICE
• FRESHLY GROUND BLACK	VINEGAR
PEPPER	• 2 TSP SUGAR
• 2 LB BONELESS SIRLOIN	• 1 TBSP VEGETABLE OIL
	• ¼ TSP CRUSHED RED
	PEPPER FLAKES

1 In a dry frying pan, toast sesame seeds over low heat, stirring almost constantly, until they are golden. Remove from frying pan and combine with sesame oil, ginger, garlic, scallion, honey to taste, soy sauce, and pepper to taste.

2 Cut steak into 1-inch cubes. Add sirloin to soy sauce blend and marinate at least 2 hours in the refrigerator. While sirloin is marinating, soak bamboo skewers in cold water.

3 To make White Radish Salad, toss white radish and carrot together. Combine with dressing made of lemon juice, soy sauce, sesame oil, rice vinegar, sugar, vegetable oil, and crushed red pepper flakes.

4 Thread 2 or 3 beef cubes onto each skewer and broil (either over hot coals or in stove broiler) until beef is cooked to desired doneness. Return beef to marinade until serving.

5 To serve, drain White Radish Salad and mound onto the center of a round serving dish. Arrange Grilled Sesame Sirloin, in spoke fashion, with points aimed at center of the dish. Serve either warm or tepid.

SERVES 8 TO 12

Note

To prevent tips of bamboo skewers from turning color during broiling, cover them with foil.

73

Pork Satay with Peanut Sauce

Pork Satay with Peanut Sauce is the classic Indonesian and Thai answer to appetizers. Despite its rather exotic sound, everyone who tries it likes it.

1 Combine *nam pla* or soy sauce, vegetable oil, lime juice, garlic, brown sugar, coriander, and cumin. Cut pork across the grain into ¼-inch-thick slices, 3 to 5 inches long. Pound a little with a mallet to tenderize. Add pork to *nam pla* mixture and marinate at least 2 hours in the refrigerator.

2 While pork is marinating, make peanut sauce by combining peanut butter, coconut milk, brown sugar, and cayenne pepper in a small saucepan. Heat just until hot to the touch. Do not allow to simmer or boil or sauce will separate. You will have 1¼ cups.

3 Soak bamboo skewers in cold water for at least 1 hour. Thread pork slices onto skewers and broil (either over hot coals or in stove broiler) until pork is cooked through. Serve hot with a bowl of peanut sauce (served tepid) for dipping.

SERVES 6 TO 10

Note

Nam pla is available in Thai or oriental food stores. Peanut Sauce can be made several days in advance but will thicken in the refrigerator. To thin, reheat over very low heat, stirring constantly. Do not allow to boil. If it still is not the desired consistency, add a little more coconut milk, 1 tablespoon at a time.

● 1 TBSP *NAM PLA* (FISH SAUCE) OR SOY SAUCE	**PEANUT SAUCE**
● 1 TBSP VEGETABLE OIL	● ½ CUP PEANUT BUTTER, EITHER SMOOTH OR CRUNCHY
● JUICE OF 1 LIME	
● 2 CLOVES GARLIC, MINCED	● ¾ CUP COCONUT MILK
● 1 TBSP BROWN SUGAR	● 1 TBSP PLUS 2 TSP BROWN SUGAR
● 1 TSP GROUND CORIANDER	
● ¼ TSP GROUND CUMIN	● ⅛ TO ¼ TSP CAYENNE PEPPER
● 1 LB (TRIMMED AND BONED) CENTER-CUT PORK CHOPS ABOUT 1½ IN. THICK	

Opposite: Pesto Pull-apart Bread (recipe on page 116); and Bloody Mary (recipe on page 18).

Southwestern Pecans

Make an extra batch of these chili- and cumin-flavored nuts and store them in the freezer. They're great to have around whenever friends stop by.

1 Preheat oven to 300 degrees. Melt butter in large skillet. Add chili powder, cumin, and garlic salt and stir to mix. Add pecans and stir well to coat the nuts.

2 Line a cookie sheet with foil and pour nuts out onto foil, spreading out on the sheet. Bake for 30 minutes, stirring occasionally. Remove from oven and sprinkle with salt to taste. Serve warm or at room temperature.

SERVES 16

● 4 TBSP BUTTER	● ⅛ TSP GARLIC SALT
● 1 TBSP CHILI POWDER	● 1 LB PECAN HALVES
● ¼ TSP GROUND CUMIN	● SALT TO TASTE

Opposite: Four-cheese torte (recipe on page 86).

75

Barbecued Chicken Wings

● 1 TBSP VEGETABLE OIL	● ¼ CUP HONEY
● 1 LARGE CLOVE GARLIC,	● 2 TBSP SOY SAUCE
MINCED	● ¼ TSP FRESHLY GROUND
● 2 TSP GROUND GINGER	BLACK PEPPER
● 2 TBSP TOMATO PASTE	● 15 CHICKEN WINGS, TIPS
● 3 TBSP LEMON JUICE	REMOVED
● 2 TBSP ORANGE JUICE	

1 Heat oil in a small saucepan. Sauté garlic over low heat for 5 minutes. Add ginger, tomato paste, lemon juice, orange juice, honey, soy sauce, and black pepper. Simmer over low heat 15 minutes.

2 Meanwhile, cut each chicken wing into 2 parts. Place in nonaluminum bowl. Pour tomato mixture over chicken and toss gently, but well. Marinate chicken in sauce 1 to 2 hours (if making on a warm day, refrigerate), stirring occasionally.

3 Preheat oven to 400 degrees. Place a rectangular cake rack on top of shallow roasting pan that has been lined with foil. Place chicken wings on the rack. Brush generously with sauce.

4 Roast 10 minutes. Turn chicken pieces over, brush again with sauce and cook 10 minutes more. Turn heat up to 550 degrees or to broil. Brush chicken pieces once more with sauce and cook another 2 to 3 minutes, until chicken is well browned. Serve the chicken hot, tepid, or cold.

SERVES 15

Cold Turkey

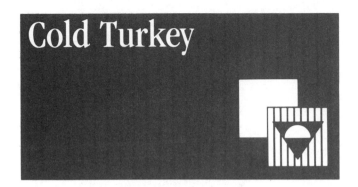

● 1 TURKEY BREAST (ABOUT	● ½ TSP CRUSHED DRIED
5½ LB), THAWED IF	THYME
FROZEN, SKINNED	● ¼ TSP CRUSHED DRIED
● 4 OZ WESTPHALIAN HAM	OREGANO
● 4 OZ SWISS CHEESE	● 1 TBSP BUTTER
● 2 TBSP DRY VERMOUTH	● ASSORTED MUSTARDS

1 Preheat oven to 325 degrees. Bone turkey breast into 2 breast halves (save bones for turkey stock if desired). Trim well. (The breast will look neater if the long, thin fillet with its white tendon is removed. This can be cut into chunks and used for turkey soup or salad if cooked.) Each trimmed breast half should weigh about 1 pound.

2 Work with one breast half at a time. Place a sharp knife at the thick side of the breast and make a deep pocket along the thick side. Be careful not to cut through the flesh. Cut ham and cheese into strips. Add half the ham and half the cheese to the pocket. Loosely sew up pocket with needle and thread. Repeat with second breast half.

3 Place each turkey breast half on a separate piece of heavy-duty aluminum foil large enough to enclose the turkey with some air space. Pour half the vermouth over each piece of turkey. Top each turkey with half the thyme and oregano. Cut butter into slivers and divide between turkey parcels.

4 Bring edges of each piece of foil up over turkey and fold, so each parcel is enclosed with room for steam. Place parcels on cookie sheet. Bake for 45 to 50 minutes. Remove from oven and let sit in foil for 15 minutes to firm up.

5 Remove from foil and chill, covered, in the refrigerator 3 to 4 hours. Using a very sharp knife, slice ⅛ to ¼ inch thick. Remove thread from slices and arrange turkey on serving platter with mustards.

SERVES 16

Mushroom and Red Wine Strudel with Sour Cream

● 1 LB FRESH MUSHROOMS	● HOT PEPPER SAUCE
● ½ CUP PLUS 2 TBSP BUTTER	● 2 OZ PHYLLO DOUGH
● ½ CUP FINELY CHOPPED	● 2 TBSP BREAD CRUMBS
ONION	● 1 CUP SOUR CREAM
● 2 TBSP LEMON JUICE	● 3 TBSP HEAVY CREAM
● ½ TSP SALT	● 1 TSP CHOPPED FRESH
● FRESHLY GROUND BLACK	CHIVES
PEPPER	
● 6 OZ (¾ CUP) DRY RED	
WINE	

This is one of the best uses for mushrooms we know. First the mushrooms are sautéed and rid of their juices, then they are scented with red wine, wrapped in flaky phyllo dough, and doused with butter. Guests will demand more of this Mushroom and Red Wine Strudel with Sour Cream.

1 Wipe mushrooms clean with paper towels. Melt 2 tablespoons butter in a large frying pan and sauté onion until soft. Finely chop mushrooms and add to frying pan. Cook mushrooms over moderate heat, stirring occasionally, until mushrooms give up their moisture and that moisture has evaporated. This probably will take about 20 minutes. Preheat oven to 350 degrees.

2 Add lemon juice, salt, pepper to taste, and red wine. Cook over moderate heat until mushrooms are very dry. Season to taste with hot pepper sauce to make mixture slightly spicy.

3 Melt remaining ½ cup butter and cool a little. On a damp kitchen towel, place 2 sheets of phyllo. Sprinkle liberally with butter. Add 2 more sheets and sprinkle with more butter. Top with 2 more sheets and sprinkle with butter. Sprinkle evenly with bread crumbs.

4 Place filling along one edge of dough, leaving about 3 inches of space on either side. Lift towel slightly and allow dough to roll 2 full turns. Tuck sides of dough toward center and continue rolling until strudel is shaped something like a large cigar.

5 Roll onto greased jellyroll pan, making sure seam end is on the bottom. Cut a few slits in the top of strudel to allow steam to escape. Sprinkle liberally with butter and bake for 40 minutes or until golden. If dough is not golden after 40 minutes, turn oven heat to broil and place under broiler for a few seconds until strudel is golden. Watch carefully; it will brown very quickly.

6 Serve strudel hot or warm with sour cream thinned with heavy cream and sprinkled with fresh chives.

SERVES 4 TO 6

Gingered Sausage

A little dried fruit, a little orange liqueur, and a lot of ginger make a sausage that really packs a punch.

1 Preheat oven to 350 degrees. In small skillet, combine dried fruit, ginger, Grand Marnier, lemon juice, brown sugar, cinnamon, and nutmeg. Simmer, covered, 15 minutes. Then mince finely by hand or in food processor.

2 Remove outer skin from sausages. Place on foil-lined cookie sheet. Spread fruit mixture over sausages. Bake for 30 minutes until fruit is firm and sausage hot. To serve, cut sausages ¼ inch thick and serve with mustard and bread.

SERVES 12

● 1½ CUPS MIXED DRIED FRUIT (APRICOTS, PEACHES, AND PRUNES ARE NICE)	● GENEROUS DASH *EACH* GROUND CINNAMON AND NUTMEG
● 1½ TSP GRATED GINGERROOT	● 1½ LB FULLY COOKED SMOKED BEEF AND PORK
● 1½ OZ (3 TBSP) GRAND MARNIER OR OTHER ORANGE-FLAVORED LIQUEUR	SAUSAGE (3 SAUSAGES, EACH ABOUT 1½ IN. IN DIAMETER, 8 IN. LONG)
	● MUSTARD
● 4 TBSP FRESH LEMON JUICE	● RYE OR PUMPERNICKEL
● 1 TBSP BROWN SUGAR	BREAD

THE WRAP UP

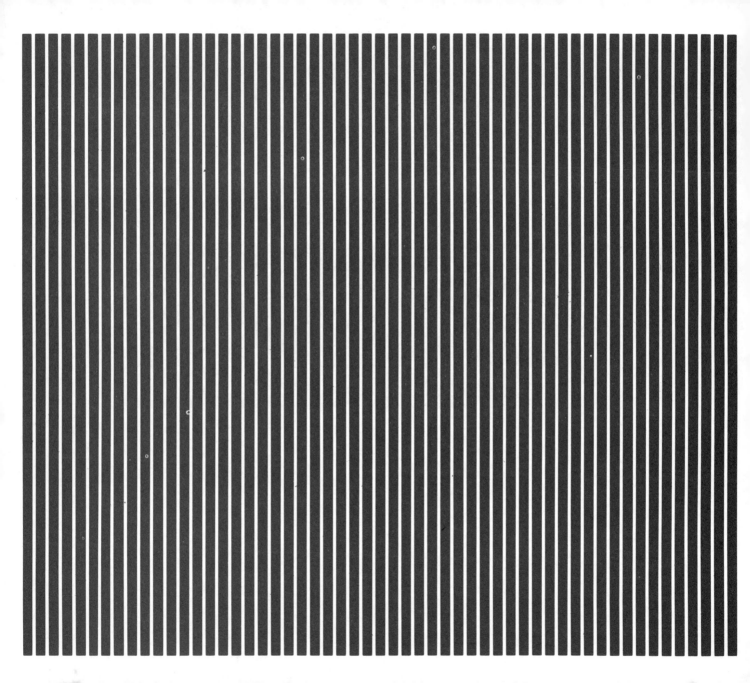

ou'll want plenty of foods packaged in pastry crust, phyllo dough, and puff pastry to make serving a breeze. The recipes in this chapter truly are finger foods.

Try our Beef and Raisin Empanadas or Leek and Cheddar Tartlets; each is a delicious mouthful.

The Four-Cheese Torte is a lovely alternative to a cheese quiche, and so easy to prepare. The Goat Cheese Mini Pizza is small enough to fit in the palm of your hand, yet hearty enough to feature as the main attraction.

Let do-it-yourselfers wrap a filling of pork and shrimp in lettuce leaves and prepare Lumpia, the Philippine version of eggrolls.

Ham and Cheese Turnovers

• 1 SHEET (8 OZ) FROZEN	• 2 TBSP MUSTARD
PUFF PASTRY	• 5 TO 6 OZ SLICED HAM
• FLOUR	• ¾ CUP GRATED GRUYÈRE
• 2 TBSP PEACH JAM	CHEESE

1 Preheat oven to 450 degrees. Thaw puff pastry. Cut the 9- to 10-inch square in half to make 2 rectangles 4½ by 9 inches. Roll half on a floured board with a floured rolling pin into a 9-inch square; trim edges. Cut that square into nine 3-inch squares.

2 Combine peach jam and mustard. Dot each square with about ¼ teaspoon peach-mustard mixture. Cut ham into 2-inch squares. Place a ham square in the center of each puff pastry square. Place a heaping teaspoon cheese in center of ham.

3 Fold the 2 opposite ends of the pastry square to the center and pinch to seal. Place on a greased cookie sheet. Repeat with remaining 8 squares. Chill while working with the second 4½-by-9-inch rectangle. Make the second 9 squares, place on the cookie sheet and chill about 15 minutes.

4 Examine turnovers before baking. If mustard has oozed out, wipe away with a damp towel. Bake for 5 minutes, reduce oven temperature to 350 degrees, and bake 10 minutes more. Remove from cookie sheet. Serve hot or tepid.

SERVES 9 TO 10

Note

If peach-mustard mixture bubbles out of turnovers during baking, it can burn. If this happens, just break off the burned parts, and no one will know the difference. Use extra peach jam-mustard combination as dipping sauce.

Four-Cheese Torte

● 1 SHEET (8 OZ) FROZEN	● ½ TSP DRIED OREGANO
PUFF PASTRY	● ⅓ CUP MINCED SCALLIONS
● FLOUR	(GREEN PART ONLY)
● 1 EGG WHITE	● ½ CUP GRATED PARMESAN
● 1 CUP GRATED MOZZARELLA	CHEESE
● ½ CUP GRATED MONTEREY	● ¼ CUP GOAT CHEESE
JACK CHEESE	● ½ TBSP OLIVE OIL

This cut-and-paste puff pastry recipe is really a work of art.

1 Thaw puff pastry. Working on floured board, cut off ⅓ of sheet (sheets are folded in thirds). Pastry should be 9 to 10 inches long and about 3 inches wide. Roll to a 10-by-5-inch rectangle, using a floured rolling pin.

2 Place the rectangle on an ungreased cookie sheet. Take the second third, and cut off 6 strips each 9 to 10 inches long and ½ inch wide. Stretch strips to 10 inches if necessary.

3 Brush the rectangle with egg white. Place one 10-inch strip along each long side of the rectangle. Brush these strips with egg white and place second strip on top of first one to create a wall along the length of 2 sides of the rectangle.

4 Cut remaining two 10-inch strips into four 4-inch lengths. Set scraps aside. Brush ends of rectangle with egg white. Place one 4-inch strip at either end, between vertical strips. Brush with egg white and top each with a second short strip. Refrigerate the puff pastry box 1 hour. Scraps and remaining puff pastry can be refrigerated several days and used for another dish.

5 Preheat oven to 350 degrees. Bake puff pastry for 20 minutes. Remove from oven. Bottom may have puffed up. Pierce with fork tines (but don't break through crust) to deflate. Press crust down. Set aside for 10 minutes to cool. Keep oven at 350 degrees.

6 Combine mozzarella and monterey jack cheese. Sprinkle half on puff pastry, keeping within borders. Sprinkle with half the oregano, crushing between fingers. Add all the scallions. Sprinkle with remaining mozzarella mixture and level mound off. Sprinkle with Parmesan. Crumble goat cheese and sprinkle over Parmesan. Crumble on remaining oregano. Drizzle with olive oil. Bake for 20 minutes or until cheese melts. Allow to set for 5 minutes, then cut into strips and serve hot.

SERVES 6 TO 8

Goat Cheese Mini Pizzas

● 1 PACKAGE ACTIVE DRY YEAST	● ¼ CUP TOMATO PASTE
	● 1 TSP DRIED BASIL
● ¼ TSP SUGAR	● ⅛ TSP FRESHLY GROUND BLACK PEPPER
● ¾ CUP WARM WATER	
● 2 CUPS PLUS 2 TBSP ALL-PURPOSE FLOUR	● 1 LARGE OR 2 SMALL GREEN BELL PEPPERS
● 1¼ TSP SALT	● 2 TBSP CORNMEAL
● 3 TBSP OLIVE OIL	● 1 PIECE FIRM GOAT CHEESE (ABOUT 2½ OZ, 2 IN. IN DIAMETER)
● 1 LARGE CLOVE GARLIC	
● 1 CAN (15 OZ) TOMATO SAUCE WITH TOMATO BITS	

Mini pizzas that fit into the palm of the hand are just right for parties. Hold a glass of Sangria in the other hand and it's a balanced snack.

1 Combine yeast, sugar, and ¼ cup warm water in a cup. Stir to dissolve yeast and set aside for 5 minutes, until yeast becomes foamy.

2 Meanwhile, combine 1 cup flour and 1 teaspoon salt in a large bowl. Make a well in the center and pour in the remaining ½ cup warm water and 1 tablespoon olive oil. Stir in yeast mixture. Stir in flour from the sides to form wet dough.

3 Stir briskly with a wooden spoon for a minute. Start adding flour, a tablespoon at a time, until dough reaches a consistency that can be kneaded. Turn out onto well-floured board and knead until dough is elastic and firm, incorporating more flour if necessary. (This dough is less sticky than the one for Calzone.)

4 Place in lightly greased bowl, turning to grease all sides. Cover bowl with towel and place in warm spot to rise for 1 hour.

5 Meanwhile, mash garlic to a pulp with remaining ¼ teaspoon salt. Heat 1 tablespoon olive oil in skillet or saucepan. Add garlic and sauté over low heat 5 minutes. Do not let garlic burn. Add tomato sauce, tomato paste, basil, and pepper. Cover and simmer for 15 minutes. Set aside.

6 Core and seed pepper. Cut into strips about 2 inches long and ¼ inch wide. Sauté pepper in remaining 1 tablespoon olive oil in medium skillet

over low heat for 10 minutes or until tender, but not browned. Set aside.

7 Preheat oven to 400 degrees. Turn dough out onto floured board and punch down. Divide into 9 equal pieces. Using floured rolling pin, roll each piece into a 4-inch circle. Place on cookie sheet dusted with cornmeal. Bake in preheated oven for 5 minutes. Dough has a tendency to puff up. Pierce with a fork to deflate. Remove from oven.

8 Spread tomato mixture evenly over pizza dough, just to the edges. Arrange 4 green pepper strips in a diamond-shape on the borders of each pizza. Slice goat cheese into 9 slices. Place each slice goat cheese in the center of the green border. Return pizzas to 400-degree oven for 10 to 15 minutes, until cheese is heated through and soft. Serve hot or warm.

SERVES 9

Mushrooming Cheese Puffs

• 2 TBSP CLARIFIED BUTTER	• 12 TO 13 SLICES COCKTAIL
• 1 SHALLOT, PEELED AND	WHITE BREAD (ABOUT
MINCED	2½-IN. SQUARES OR
• ½ LB MUSHROOMS,	ROUNDS)
CLEANED WITH STEMS	• 1 PACKED CUP GRATED
TRIMMED	GRUYÈRE CHEESE
• 1 TSP LEMON JUICE	• 1 EGG, BEATEN
• SALT AND WHITE PEPPER	• ½ CUP HEAVY CREAM
• BUTTER	• PINCH OF NUTMEG

Use this mushroom mixture to stuff a mushroom cap, fill a crêpe, or provide a layer for the creamy sandwich that follows.

1 Heat clarified butter in medium skillet. Add shallot and cook over low heat 5 minutes.

2 Meanwhile, finely mince mushrooms by hand and add to skillet. Cook, stirring occasionally, about 20 minutes or until mushrooms are tender and dry. Mushrooms will at first give off liquid which will evaporate. Stir in lemon juice, and salt and pepper to taste. Set aside to cool.

3 Preheat oven to 550 degrees. Butter bread on one side and place on ungreased cookie sheet. Spoon 1 rounded tablespoon mushroom mixture on each piece of bread.

4 Combine grated cheese, egg, cream, nutmeg, and salt and pepper to taste. Carefully spoon over mushroom mixture, allowing 1 generous tablespoon per sandwich. Bake for 3 to 5 minutes, until cheese mixture is lightly browned. Serve hot.

SERVES 12 TO 13

Note
Mushroom mixture can be made well in advance and frozen several months or refrigerated for a few days. Sandwiches can be reheated, but are better fresh. To reheat, place on ungreased cookie sheet, cover loosely with foil, and place in preheated 325 degree oven for 10 minutes.

Opposite: Goat Cheese Mini Pizzas (recipe on page 88).

Phyllo Bundles Filled with Spinach and Cheese

Phyllo Bundles are miniature versions of the famous Greek dish, *spanakopita*. Using commercially prepared phyllo dough makes them easy to prepare. Remember to move swiftly when working with commercially prepared phyllo. It dries out quickly.

● 1 PACKAGE (10 OZ) FROZEN	● ¼ CUP CRUMBLED RICOTTA
CHOPPED SPINACH,	CHEESE
DEFROSTED AND SQUEEZED	● ½ CUP GRATED PARMESAN
DRY	CHEESE
● 2 SCALLIONS, BOTH GREEN	● 8 OZ PHYLLO DOUGH
AND WHITE PARTS SLICED	● 1 CUP BUTTER, MELTED
● 1 CUP CRUMBLED FETA	● FRESH SPINACH, WASHED
CHEESE	AND DRIED THOROUGHLY

1 Preheat oven to 425 degrees. Combine spinach, scallions, and cheeses. Lay 2 sheets of phyllo dough, one on top of the other, on a board. (Keep remaining sheets covered with a slightly damp cloth.) Brush generously with melted butter. Cut into strips 4 inches wide, 7 inches long. Place about 1 teaspoon of filling on one end of each strip. Fold sides toward center, then fold end to make a square. Allow some air space inside so that filling has room to expand during baking. Continue folding until one strip of phyllo is used and spinach is wrapped in small square phyllo packet. Press edges of dough in to seal, using more butter.

2 Repeat making squares with remaining strips and filling. Butter tops of bundles, pierce several times with a knife so that steam can escape, and place on an ungreased cookie sheet. Bake for 5 minutes. Turn up heat to broil and place in broiler for a minute or two until bundles are golden. Serve hot or tepid.

SERVES ABOUT 15

Opposite: Tanqueray and Tonic (recipe on page 24).

Leek and Cheddar Tartlets

● PASTRY CRUST (PAGE 192)	● 1 TSP PREPARED MUSTARD
● 2 LEEKS	● 1 TSP WORCESTERSHIRE
● 1½ TBSP BUTTER	SAUCE
● 4 OZ SHARP CHEDDAR	● SALT AND WHITE PEPPER
CHEESE, SHREDDED	● 24 PIMIENTO-STUFFED
● 2 EGG YOLKS	OLIVES
● ½ CUP HEAVY CREAM,	
APPROXIMATELY	

This tartlet is small enough to be only a mouthful—but what a mouthful. Make extras; these are very popular and go fast.

1 Prepare pastry. Wrap in plastic wrap and chill 30 minutes before using.

2 Preheat oven to 350 degrees. Prepare filling. Trim stem ends off leeks. Remove green part. Slice white stalks vertically in 2 and rinse under running water. Pat dry and mince coarsely by hand or in food processor.

3 Melt butter in medium skillet. Sauté leeks over low heat about 10 minutes, until tender, but not browned. Allow leeks to cool.

4 In a bowl, combine cheddar, egg yolks, ½ cup cream, prepared mustard, Worcestershire, and salt and pepper to taste. Stir in leeks. If mixture seems dry rather than creamy, add 1 to 2 more tablespoons cream. Set aside.

5 There is enough pastry and filling for 24 mini-muffin pans or tart shells with a 1½-inch diameter. It may be easier to work with half the dough at a time.

6 On a floured board, using a floured rolling pin, roll out dough to 1/16-inch thickness. Cut into 3-inch rounds. Fit dough into ungreased mini-muffin pans, pleating edges 2 or 3 times to fit dough and form an attractive floral shape. Rework scraps to make more crust. If dough becomes sticky, refrigerate pastry before filling and baking.

7 Spoon a scant tablespoon filling into each pastry. Bake for 20 to 25 minutes or until filling is puffy and lightly browned.

8 Allow tartlets to cool in pans 5 minutes, then remove to rack to cool completely. Slice each olive into thirds. Place 3 slices on top of each tartlet.

SERVES 12

Note

These can be rewarmed (store, covered in the refrigerator up to 2 days), but shouldn't be frozen.

Onion and Bacon Tart

The sweetness of onions fried with butter mingled with the saltiness of bacon makes this a delicious, rich tart. It's inspired by a well-known creation from the Alsace region of France.

1 Preheat oven to 350 degrees. Sauté onions in butter until onions are soft. Turn up heat and fry, stirring often, until onions are golden. Do not allow to turn dark brown. Sauté bacon until crispy. Drain and crumble into bits.

2 Line a 9-inch tart pan with pastry. Prick with a fork and bake for 8 to 10 minutes or until pastry begins to turn color. Remove from oven and cool.

3 Combine eggs, salt, cream, and mustard. Spread onions in an even layer on bottom of pie crust. Pour egg/cream mixture over, sprinkle evenly with bacon, and bake 40 minutes or until golden. Allow to cool for at least 15 minutes before slicing. Serve hot or tepid.

SERVES 6 TO 8

● 6 CUPS SLICED ONIONS	● 2 EGGS, LIGHTLY BEATEN
● 6 TBSP BUTTER	● ½ TSP SALT
● 6 SLICES BACON	● ½ CUP HEAVY CREAM
● PASTRY FOR A 9-IN. TART PAN (PAGE 192)	● 2 TBSP DIJON-STYLE MUSTARD

Garlic Sausage in Pastry

Garlic Sausage in Pastry with honey mustard is good for cocktail parties and also as an entree. With steamed vegetables or a salad, it serves 3 to 4 for a light dinner.

1 Preheat oven to 425 degrees. Thaw puff pastry. Remove casing from sausage by making shallow slashes from end to end. Slowly peel off casing. Roll pastry 1/8 inch thick and large enough to cover sausage. Sprinkle pastry liberally with pepper. Place sausage in center and fold sides up to cover. Trim off excess and reserve. Press sides together to seal. Pastry will look like a cylinder. Fold remaining 2 open ends under and press to seal on bottom where sides are sealed.

2 Brush sausage with beaten egg and set, folded side on the bottom, on an ungreased cookie sheet. Use remaining pastry to make decorations on top. Brush decorations with beaten egg. Bake 25 minutes or until golden.

3 While sausage is baking, combine mustard and honey. When sausage is golden, remove from oven. Slice and serve warm or tepid with honey mustard on the side.

SERVES 8 TO 10

• 1 SHEET (8 OZ) FROZEN	• 1 EGG, LIGHTLY BEATEN
PUFF PASTRY	• 1/2 CUP DIJON-STYLE
• 1 COOKED (12 OZ) GARLIC	MUSTARD
SAUSAGE	• 3 TBSP HONEY
• FRESHLY GROUND BLACK	
PEPPER	

Beef and Raisin Empanadas

● ¼ CUP CHOPPED ONION	● 3 TBSP RAISINS
● 1 TBSP BUTTER	● ¾ CUP COOKED GROUND
● 1 TSP GROUND CUMIN	BEEF
● 1 TBSP CURRY POWDER	● PASTRY FOR TWO 9-IN. PIE
● 1 TBSP TOMATO PASTE	CRUSTS (PAGE 192)
● ¼ CUP HEAVY CREAM	● 1 EGG WHITE, BEATEN

1 Preheat oven to 350 degrees. Sauté the onion in butter until soft. Add cumin and curry powder and cook for 30 seconds, stirring constantly. Add tomato paste, cream, and raisins and cook until cream is thick, stirring constantly. Add cooked beef and continue to cook until mixture is almost dry. Cool.

2 Roll out pastry to ⅛-inch thickness, and cut into rounds that are 2½ inches in diameter. Place about 1 teaspoon of filling into center of each round and pinch edges of dough together to form half circles. Repeat until all filling is used, using a little egg white to help seal shut if necessary. Brush each with egg white and bake for 25 minutes or until golden. Serve hot or tepid.

SERVES 8 TO 12

Lumpia

● 1 PACKAGE (6 OZ) COOKED	● 1 CUP FRESH BEAN SPROUTS
FROZEN BABY SHRIMP,	● ¼ TSP SALT
THAWED	● ¼ TSP FRESHLY GROUND
● 1 TBSP VEGETABLE OIL	BLACK PEPPER
● ¼ LB FRESH PORK SAUSAGE	● 20 TO 24 BIBB LETTUCE
● 1 CLOVE GARLIC, PEELED	LEAVES
AND MINCED	● SLIGHTLY SOUR APRICOT
● 1 MEDIUM-SIZED ONION,	SAUCE (PAGE 130)
PEELED AND DICED	
● 2 CUPS MINCED CHINESE	
CABBAGE	

This version of the Philippine eggroll uses lettuce as a wrapper. Small Bibb lettuce leaves make just the right sized container. In this recipe the leaves are steamed to make them more pliable; however they can be served raw and crisp as well.

1 Drain shrimp and set aside. Heat oil in a large skillet. Add sausage, garlic, and onion and sauté about 10 minutes, until all the pink is gone from the sausage. Break sausage up with a spoon while cooking.

2 Add Chinese cabbage, bean sprouts, salt, and pepper. Cook about 3 to 5 minutes more, until vegetables are tender-crisp. Stir in shrimp and heat through. Keep warm.

3 Wash lettuce and pat dry. Steam for 30 seconds, then arrange lettuce leaves on large serving platter. Divide mixture among lettuce leaves. Either serve Lumpia in open lettuce cups and allow guests to fold them, or do it before serving. Bring sides of each lettuce leaf to the center, then roll up. Place seam-side down on serving platter. Serve warm or tepid with sauce.

SERVES 24

Note

Do not make these in advance or they will become very soggy.

FOODS THAT COME IN FROM THE COLD

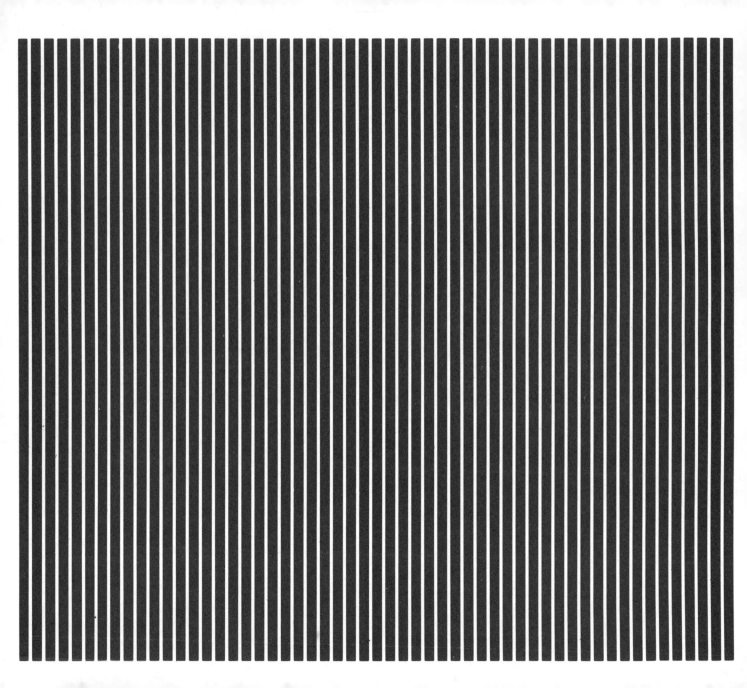

Is it possible to set a bountiful table without heating up the house? It's not only possible, it's a snap using our array of no-cook dishes.

Make Gravlax, a cured salmon delicacy; Dilly Cucumber Salad, a crisp sweet-sour relish; and Bean and Leek Terrine, a creamy, slightly piquant mold. Keep a jar of Marinated Green Olives around.

Use the refrigerator instead of the oven and you'll stay as cool as the foods.

A Salmon Caper

● 1 ENVELOPE UNFLAVORED	● 1 TBSP CAPERS
GELATIN	● 1 CAN (15½ OZ) RED
● ¼ CUP COLD WATER	SALMON, OR 2 CUPS
● ½ CUP BOILING WATER	COOKED SALMON
● ¼ CUP MAYONNAISE	● ½ CUP HEAVY CREAM
● ¼ CUP SOUR CREAM	● 2 ROUNDED TBSP RED
● 1 TBSP GRATED OR PURÉED	CAVIAR (OPTIONAL)
ONION	● DILLY CUCUMBER SALAD
● 1 TSP GOOD-QUALITY	(PAGE 104)
PAPRIKA	

1 Soften gelatin in cold water. Add boiling water and stir to dissolve. Cool. Add mayonnaise, sour cream, grated onion, and paprika. Whisk well. Stir in capers.

2 Drain canned salmon. Remove skin and bones from canned (or fresh) salmon. Mash finely with fork (or use food processor, being careful not to overprocess).

3 Stir salmon into gelatin mixture. Whip cream until stiff. Fold in salmon mixture. Gently fold in caviar if desired. Spoon into well-buttered 5-cup ring mold. Chill in refrigerator 3 to 4 hours, until set. Unmold onto serving platter and place a bowl of Dilly Cucumber Salad in the center.

SERVES 8

Dilly Cucumber Salad

1 Combine cucumber and onion slices in glass bowl. Add salt and toss well. Set aside for 2 hours. Rinse under cold water and drain well.

2 Return cucumbers and onions to glass bowl. Toss with dill. In small saucepan, combine 5 tablespoons vinegar with sugar. Heat until sugar dissolves. Taste. If mixture isn't sharp enough add another tablespoon vinegar. Pour over cucumbers and toss well. Refrigerate until well chilled, about 2 to 3 hours. Serve with A Salmon Caper.

SERVES 8

● 2 MEDIUM CUCUMBERS, THINLY SLICED	● 1 TBSP MINCED FRESH DILL
● 1 SMALL ONION, PEELED AND THINLY SLICED	● 5 TO 6 TBSP WHITE WINE VINEGAR
● 1 TBSP COARSE SALT	● 2 TBSP SUGAR
	● A SALMON CAPER (PAGE 103)

Marinated Goat Cheese

● 8 OZ MILD GOAT CHEESE	● 2 TBSP MINCED FRESH
(MONTRACHET IS GOOD)	BASIL OR DILL
● 1½ CUPS OLIVE OIL	● 2 BAY LEAVES
● 3 CLOVES GARLIC, MINCED	● FRESHLY GROUND BLACK
● 2 TSP FRESH MARJORAM	PEPPER

To best enjoy the flavors of Marinated Goat Cheese, serve it with chunks of sourdough bread and drizzle a bit of the marinade on the bread.

1 With a very sharp knife, slice cheese into ¾-inch-thick rounds.

2 Combine olive oil, garlic, marjoram, basil or dill, and bay leaves, and season with lots of pepper. Add cheese. Cover and marinate overnight in the refrigerator. Do not marinate longer than 24 hours. Serve tepid.

SERVES 6 TO 8

Gravlax

● 1 BUNCH FRESH DILL	● 1 TSP LEMON JUICE
● 1½ LB FINEST QUALITY	● BUTTERED COCKTAIL RYE
FRESH SALMON FILLET	BREAD
● ¼ CUP SALT	● LEMON WEDGES AND DILL
● ½ CUP SUGAR	SPRIGS
● 1 TBSP CRUSHED WHITE	
PEPPERCORNS	

This salt- and sugar-cured salmon dish has a refreshing briny taste. Since the salmon is never really cooked, it must be absolutely fresh.

1 Stem dill and coarsely chop to yield about ½ cup. Place half the dill in the bottom of an oval glass or ceramic casserole. Place fish, skin side down, on top of dill. Mix together salt, sugar, and peppercorns and sprinkle over fish. Sprinkle with lemon juice. Cover with remaining dill.

2 Cover tightly with plastic wrap. Then place heavy weights (1-pound cans are fine) over salmon. Refrigerate. Juices will form in the casserole. Check salmon every few hours and spoon juices back over the fish.

3 Keep refrigerated 24 to 36 hours, then scrape dill, sugar, salt, and peppercorns off salmon. Using very sharp knife, cut salmon thinly on the diagonal leaving skin behind. Arrange on a platter with buttered bread and garnish with dill sprigs and lemon wedges.

SERVES 10

Note
Before preparing dish, run a finger down the fillet against the grain to check for bones. Remove these with a strawberry huller or tweezer.

Opposite: Gravlox; and Iced Chili Vodka (recipe on page 17). Following pages: Irish Coffee (recipe on page 22). Cheese and Pepperoni Ring (recipe on page 115); and Marguerita (recipe on page 21). Tiny Black Walnut Bran Muffins (recipe on page 117).

Marinated Green Olives

1 Combine olives, olive oil, garlic, and onion in a jar.

2 Cover tightly and refrigerate for a minimum of 48 hours, shaking jar occasionally to blend ingredients. Olives can begin marinating several weeks in advance. Serve tepid.

SERVES 6 TO 8

● 1 JAR (13 OZ) GREEN	● 6 CLOVES GARLIC, PEELED
OLIVES WITH PITS,	AND SLIGHTLY CRUSHED
DRAINED AND LIGHTLY	● ¼ CUP THINLY SLICED
CRUSHED	ONION
● ½ CUP OLIVE OIL	

Bean and Leek Terrine

● 3 CUPS COOKED GREAT NORTHERN WHITE BEANS	● 2 TBSP MINCED PARSLEY
● 3 LEEKS	● ½ TO 1 TSP SALT
● 1 SMALL ONION, PEELED AND MINCED	● FRESHLY GROUND WHITE PEPPER
● ½ CUP BUTTER	● 2 ENVELOPES UNFLAVORED GELATIN
● 1 CUP SOUR CREAM	● ⅓ CUP DRY WHITE WINE
● ⅓ CUP CHOPPED FRESH CHIVES	

1 Rinse beans in water and set aside to drain. Cut leeks in half lengthwise and wash well under cold, running water. Trim green part of leeks from white part. Boil leek greens in water for 15 minutes or until tender. Drain and set aside.

2 Mince white part of leek and sauté with onion in butter until onion is tender. Cool.

3 Purée beans and sour cream in batches in food processor or blender until beans are as smooth as possible. By hand, fold in leek and onion mixture, chives, parsley, salt, and white pepper to taste. Soften gelatin in white wine for a minute. Heat until gelatin is dissolved. Cool and fold into bean mixture.

4 Pat green part of leeks dry and use to line an oiled 5-cup loaf terrine. Allow about 3 inches of leek to extend over edges of the terrine. Pour bean mixture in and smooth top with a knife. Cover and refrigerate 5 to 6 hours or until firm.

5 To unmold, lower terrine into very warm water almost up to the top of the terrine. Count to 10. Remove from water, dry terrine, fold leek ends over top, cover with serving dish, and quickly invert terrine and dish. If loaf does not drop out onto dish, repeat water dunking. It probably will take several such water baths for loaf to melt enough around the edges so that it drops out of the terrine. Slice and serve cold.

SERVES 12 TO 14

Fruit Punch

This one isn't a beverage, but a socko fruit salad that's for adults only. Provide either toothpicks or small cocktail forks for spearing the fruit.

1 Peel bananas and slice into 1-inch chunks. Sprinkle with lemon juice.

2 Place bananas in a serving bowl with the pineapple chunks. Combine ginger, grenadine, and Grand Marnier. Pour over fruit. Mix gently but well. Chill 1 to 3 hours.

3 Arrange mint sprigs or leaves around fruit as a garnish and serve fruit cold.

SERVES 8

● 2 LARGE RIPE BANANAS	● 4 OZ (½ CUP) GRAND
● 1 TBSP LEMON JUICE	MARNIER OR OTHER
● 2 CUPS FRESH, PEELED	ORANGE-FLAVORED
PINEAPPLE CHUNKS	LIQUEUR
● 2 TSP GRATED GINGERROOT	● MINT SPRIGS
● 2 TSP GRENADINE	

NOT THE YEAST OF THEM

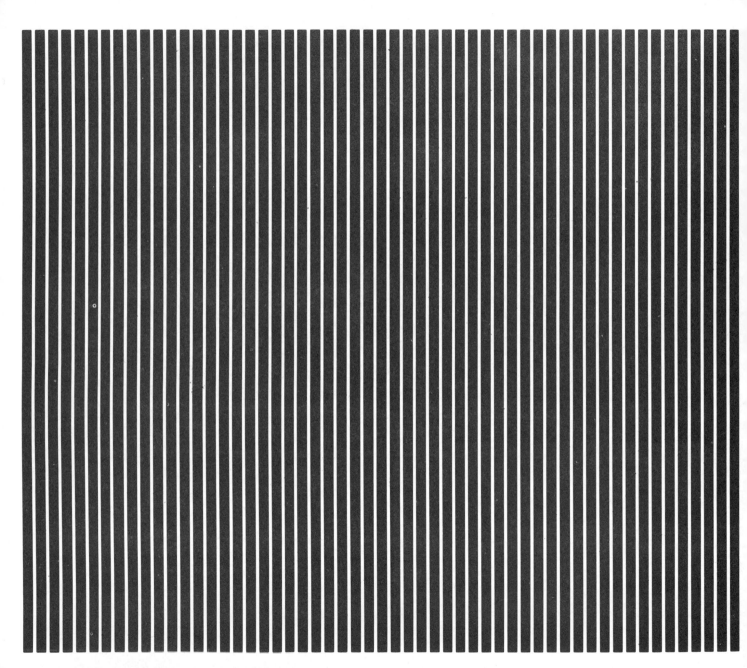

rotestations aside, people are eating breads—even at cocktail parties.

Stay away from the cottony stuff and show guests how good home-baked bread can taste.

Nothing can take the place of a warm, chewy Braided Whole Wheat Molasses Bread or Buttery Corn Bread Sticks.

Prepare Tiny Black Walnut Muffins, rich and deeply flavored, or lacy and zesty Indian Pepper Bread. Make a basic puff pastry, but add pepperoni for a pungent taste.

Set a Pesto Pull-Apart Bread on the table as a centerpiece. It's proof that bread is the staff of (party) life.

Cheese and Pepperoni Ring

Serve this flavorful cheese and meat ring plain or add a small platter of sliced pepperoni to the center of the dish.

1 Preheat oven to 400 degrees. Combine milk and butter in heavy-bottomed saucepan. Bring to a boil. Add flour all at once. Reduce heat to simmer and stir vigorously until mixture is smooth and comes away from sides of pan. Turn off heat and cool mixture 5 minutes.

2 Beat in eggs, one at a time, beating well after each addition, until eggs are incorporated. Stir in cheese and pepperoni.

3 Using a tablespoon, heap mixture onto greased and floured cookie sheet, forming a 9-inch circle. Brush top of ring with egg white. Bake for 10 minutes. Reduce heat to 350 degrees and then bake for 30 minutes more. Turn off oven and allow to rest 10 minutes. Remove from oven and serve hot or tepid.

SERVES 10

• 1 CUP MILK	• 1 CUP GRATED GRUYÈRE
• ½ CUP BUTTER, DICED	CHEESE
• 1 CUP SIFTED ALL-PURPOSE	• 2 OUNCES GRATED
FLOUR	PEPPERONI
• 4 EGGS, AT ROOM	• 1 EGG WHITE
TEMPERATURE	

Pesto Pull-Apart Bread

● 1 CLOVE GARLIC	● 1 PACKAGE ACTIVE DRY
● ½ CUP FIRMLY PACKED	YEAST
FRESH BASIL LEAVES	● 1¼ CUPS VERY WARM
● ½ CUP GRATED ROMANO	WATER
CHEESE	● 3 CUPS ALL-PURPOSE FLOUR
● ¼ CUP OLIVE OIL	● ½ TSP SALT
● PINCH OF SUGAR	

1 Mince together garlic and basil leaves (this can also be done in a food processor fitted with a steel blade). Add romano cheese. Place in a small bowl and gradually whisk in oil, stirring constantly (if using a food processor, turn it on and drizzle the oil in). Set aside.

2 Place a generous pinch of sugar and the yeast in small bowl. Add ¼ cup warm water. Stir. Set aside 5 minutes for yeast to foam up.

3 In large bowl, place 2 cups flour and ½ teaspoon salt. Stir. Make a well in the dry ingredients. Add yeast mixture, basil mixture, and 1 cup water. Stir well. Gradually add 1 cup flour. Stir to make a kneadable dough. It may still be sticky, but that's fine. Turn out onto lightly floured board and knead until smooth and elastic, about 10 minutes. (Begin kneading process by throwing dough down on board a dozen times; this way it will require less additional flour.) Place dough in greased bowl, turning to grease all sides. Cover bowl with towel and set aside in warm place for 1 hour.

4 Punch dough down and knead briefly. Divide dough into 14 or 15 balls and fit around the edge of a 14-inch greased round cake or pizza pan, or arrange them in a free-form circle, allowing a little room between balls for rising. Cover with a towel and let rise 30 minutes in a warm place.

5 Preheat oven to 375 degrees. Place pan in oven and bake for 35 to 40 minutes or until bread is golden. Cool in pan 10 minutes, then turn out onto rack.

SERVES 14

Tiny Black Walnut Bran Muffins

● ¼ CUP BUTTER	● ½ TSP GROUND GINGER
● ⅓ CUP SUGAR	● ¼ TSP GROUND CLOVES
● 1 EGG	● ½ CUP BRAN CEREAL
● ½ CUP DARK MOLASSES	● ⅓ CUP CHOPPED BLACK
● 1½ CUPS ALL-PURPOSE	WALNUTS
FLOUR	● ¼ CUP WATER
● 1 TSP BAKING SODA	● ORANGE HONEY BUTTER
● ½ TSP GROUND CINNAMON	(PAGE 194)

1 Preheat oven to 375 degrees. Grease muffin tins that are 1½ inches in diameter.

2 Cream butter and sugar together. Add egg and molasses, and mix until thoroughly combined. Stir together flour, soda, cinnamon, ginger, and cloves. Add to butter mixture along with bran, walnuts, and water. Stir until thoroughly combined. Pour into muffin tins.

3 Bake 12 to 15 minutes or until muffins begin to brown. Let sit 5 minutes before removing muffins from pan. Serve with Orange Honey Butter.

MAKES ABOUT 30 MUFFINS

Braided Whole Wheat Molasses Bread

● ½ CUP MILK	● 1 TSP SALT
● 3 TBSP BUTTER	● 2 CUPS ALL-PURPOSE FLOUR
● 3 TBSP MOLASSES	● 1 BEATEN EGG
● 1 PACKAGE ACTIVE DRY YEAST	● ORANGE HONEY BUTTER (PAGE 194) OR CREAM
● 2 TBSP HONEY	CHEESE AND MANGO
● ¾ CUP WARM WATER	CHUTNEY (PAGE 191)
● 2½ CUPS WHOLE WHEAT FLOUR	

1 Combine milk, butter, and molasses. Bring to a boil, turn off heat, and allow to sit until it is tepid. Dissolve yeast and honey in warm water. Set aside until yeast foams.

2 Place whole wheat flour and salt in a large bowl. Add yeast mixture and milk mixture to flour, and stir to combine. Add 1½ cups all-purpose flour or enough to make a manageable dough. Turn dough out onto floured board and knead until smooth, elastic, and no longer sticky. This will take about 10 minutes.

3 Place dough in an oiled bowl, turning so that top of dough is lightly covered with oil. Cover with a towel and set in a warm place until doubled in bulk, about 1½ hours. Punch dough down and knead for several minutes. Divide dough into 6 equal parts. On a table, with hands, roll each dough part into a rope 16 inches long. (Place other pieces of dough into a plastic bag so they don't dry out.) Connect 3 dough ropes by pinching one end of each together. Braid into a long rope. Pinch ends together and place on a greased cookie sheet. Repeat with remaining dough. Place breads in a warm place and allow to rise again until doubled in bulk, about 1 hour.

4 Preheat oven to 375 degrees. Bake loaves 15 minutes, remove from oven, and brush with beaten egg. Return to oven for 5 more minutes or until breads sound hollow when tapped. Serve with Orange Honey Butter or cream cheese and Mango Chutney.

SERVES 12 TO 24

Chili Breadsticks

These breadsticks are so easy, you'll wonder why you don't make them more often.

1 Place bread dough in a plastic bag and defrost for about 2 hours at room temperature.

2 Preheat oven to 350 degrees. Using 1 tablespoon of dough per stick, roll dough with hands into pencil-thin sticks about 8 inches long. Dip each in water. Sprinkle liberally with chili powder and roll in parmesan cheese until thoroughly coated.

3 Place sticks on an ungreased cookie sheet. Repeat with remaining ingredients. Bake for 25 minutes. Serve tepid.

SERVES 8 TO 10

● 1 LB FROZEN BREAD	● ½ CUP FINELY GRATED
DOUGH	PARMESAN CHEESE
● CHILI POWDER	

Whole Wheat French Bread

● 1 PACKAGE ACTIVE DRY YEAST	● 1¼ CUPS ALL-PURPOSE FLOUR
● 1 TSP SUGAR	● 1 CUP WHOLE WHEAT FLOUR
● 1 CUP VERY WARM WATER	
● 2 TBSP OLIVE OIL	● CORNMEAL
● 1 TSP SALT	

Add a little whole wheat flour to a French bread recipe and you've got a wholesome, nutty-tasting loaf. This bread is especially good torn into chunks and dunked into the sauce of the Garlicky Shrimp dish (page 171).

1 Combine yeast, sugar, and ¼ cup warm water in a cup. Stir and set aside for 5 minutes for yeast to foam. Add olive oil, stirring in.

2. Stir together salt, 1 cup all-purpose flour, and 1 cup whole wheat flour in a large bowl. Pour in yeast mixture and remaining ¾ cup warm water. Mix well with a spoon.

3 Turn out dough onto a floured board using remaining ¼ cup all-purpose flour, and knead 10 minutes. Place dough in a greased bowl, turning to grease all sides. Cover with cloth towel. Place in a warm area to rise 1 hour.

4 Punch dough down and divide in half. Shape each half into a long loaf. Place loaves on pan dusted with cornmeal. Make one or two diagonal slashes in the top of each loaf. Cover with a towel and allow to rise again for 30 minutes.

5 Preheat the oven to 375 degrees. Bake breads for 30 minutes, or until they are golden and done. Remove from oven and cool. Serve slightly warm or cold.

SERVES 6 TO 8

Buttery Cornbread Sticks

Sometimes simple and traditional is too good to be adulterated. We've added extra butter to these cornbread sticks, though, to make them a bit richer. They're wonderful served with Irish Coffee.

1 Preheat oven to 425 degrees. Generously grease a cornstick pan. Combine cornmeal, flour, sugar, salt, and baking powder. Add egg, butter, and milk, and beat until thoroughly combined. Spoon into cornstick pan. Bake for 13 minutes or until cornbread sticks are golden. Serve with Orange Honey Butter.

MAKES ABOUT 9 STICKS

● 1 CUP YELLOW CORNMEAL	● 1 EGG
● ½ CUP ALL-PURPOSE FLOUR	● 6 TBSP BUTTER, MELTED
● ¼ CUP SUGAR	● ½ CUP MILK
● ¼ TSP SALT	● ORANGE HONEY BUTTER
● 2 TSP BAKING POWDER	(PAGE 194)

Note
To make mini-muffins, spoon cornbread batter into greased muffin tins that are 1½ inches in diameter. Bake 10 minutes or until cornbread muffins are golden. Makes about 19 muffins.

121

Indian Pepper Bread

● 1 CUP CAKE FLOUR	● 1¾ CUPS WATER
● 1 TSP SALT	● VEGETABLE OIL FOR
● 2 TO 3 TSP WHITE PEPPER	DEEP-FRYING
OR TO TASTE	

This peppery bread requires careful cooking attention, but the result is worth the effort. It's one of our most interesting creations, gleaned from travels in India.

1 Combine flour, salt, white pepper, and water. (Always stir this just before adding to frying pan.)

2 Over medium-low heat, heat ¼ inch of oil in a 9-inch nonstick frying pan. Stir batter. Measure 3 tablespoons into a cup. Stir again and quickly but gently pour into frying pan. Allow to cook for 3 minutes, then place wooden mallet or other small weight over center of bread to ensure that center cooks through. If edges burn, oil is too hot.

3 Continue frying for 3 more minutes or until bread is stiff. Flip over and replace mallet in center. Fry on this side until bread is uniformly golden, about 3 to 5 more minutes. Drain well on paper towel. Repeat with remaining batter. Serve tepid. These almost paper-thin breads are shaped something like a snowflake; they can be made several days in advance.

SERVES 8 TO 10

Opposite: Indian Pepper Bread. Following page: Braided Whole-wheat Molasses Bread (recipe on page 118); and Mulled Cinnamon Cider (recipe on page 18).

OIL'S WELL THAT BEGINS WELL

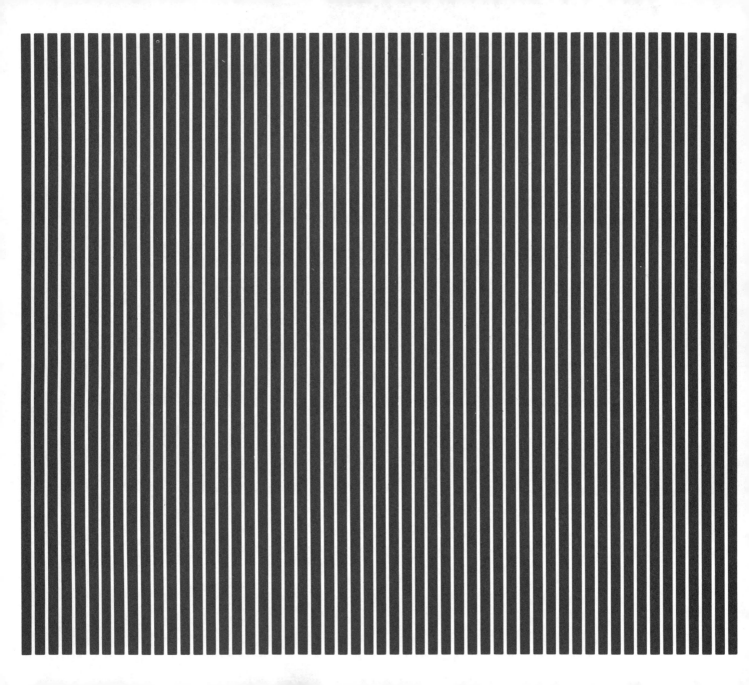

erhaps the best way to serve deep-fried foods is at a casual get-together where guests feel free to wander through the kitchen and see what's cooking.

Let them sample fiery Jalapeño Wontons, crunchy Sweet-Potato Chips, pungent Cauliflower in a Curried Beer Batter, or nourishing Calzone.

Some guests become so enthused by the crisp texture and savory flavor of freshly deep-fried foods, they volunteer to cook.

If you must make these dishes in advance, prepare them as close to party time as possible and keep them warm, uncovered, in a 200-degree oven.

A Bowl of Chips

● 3 SWEET POTATOES	● SALT
● VEGETABLE OIL FOR	
DEEP-FRYING	

1 Either peel potatoes or leave unpeeled, as desired. Slice as thin as possible (about $\frac{1}{16}$ inch thick) and soak in a bowl of cold water 1 to 2 hours.

2 Heat 1 inch of vegetable oil in a heavy-bottomed skillet or electric deep-fryer to 375 degrees. Remove potatoes from water, a few at a time, and pat dry. Drop into hot oil and fry until golden, from 1 to 3 minutes, depending on thickness of potatoes.

3 Meanwhile, line a cookie sheet with paper towels. Preheat oven to 200 degrees.

4 When potatoes are done, remove from oil with slotted spoon and place on cookie sheet. Keep warm in oven while preparing remaining potato slices. Salt potatoes and place in baskets. Serve hot.

SERVES 10

NOTE

Bananas are also excellent deep-fried. Don't soak in water. Simply slice thin and immediately fry in oil for 1 minute. These are best if cooked just before serving.

Jalapeño Wontons

● 1 PACKAGE (8 OZ)	● 3 TBSP FLOUR
CHEDDAR-FLAVORED	● VEGETABLE OIL FOR
COLD-PACK CHEESE FOOD	DEEP-FRYING
● ¼ TSP SUGAR	● 8 WONTON WRAPPERS
● 1 TSP CRUSHED RED	● 1 EGG, LIGHTLY BEATEN
PEPPER FLAKES	
● ⅛ TSP PAPRIKA	
● 4 TBSP CHOPPED AND	
DRAINED CANNED JALAPEÑO	
PEPPERS	

There's a fiery crunch in every mouthful of these wontons. The cheese filling can also be warmed in the top of a double boiler and served as a dip for taco chips.

1 Cream together cheese, sugar, pepper flakes, and paprika. Fold in jalapeño peppers and flour. Stir well. Cover and chill several hours if possible for flavors to develop.

2 Pour enough oil in deep-fryer to measure 1 inch depth. Heat to 375 degrees.

3 Meanwhile, cut each wonton wrapper into quarters. Work with 2 quarters at a time, keeping remainder covered with plastic wrap. Place a tablespoon cheese mixture in center of one quarter. Brush edges with egg. Top with a second quarter, and pinch edges to seal. Drop into hot oil, cooking 1 to 2 minutes on one side and 30 seconds to 1 minute on the second side.

4 Drain on paper towels. Repeat with remaining cheese and wonton wrappers. Fry as many wontons as the fryer will accommodate comfortably at one time. Don't crowd.

SERVES 8

Note

These reheat very well. If doing ahead, fry only until light brown. Reheat in preheated 300-degree oven for about 8 minutes.

Fried Wontons Filled with Brie and Bacon

1 Preheat oil to 375 degrees. Remove crust from brie and discard. Divide brie into 12 equal parts. Sauté bacon until crispy. Drain and crumble into bits.

2 Place a piece of brie on top of each wonton wrapper. Top each with about 1 teaspoon of crumbled bacon. Brush 2 adjacent sides of each wrapper with beaten egg, and fold wrapper over to seal into a triangular shape.

3 Deep-fry wontons in hot oil until golden. Drain on paper towels, then serve hot with Mango Chutney.

SERVES 6

● VEGETABLE OIL FOR	● 12 WONTON WRAPPERS
DEEP-FRYING	● 1 BEATEN EGG
● 4½ OZ BRIE CHEESE	● MANGO CHUTNEY (PAGE
● 4 SLICES BACON	191)

Eggrolls with Slightly Sour Apricot Sauce

● 6 DRIED BLACK MUSHROOMS	● 4 SCALLIONS, BOTH WHITE AND GREEN PARTS SHREDDED
● 1 TSP SESAME OIL	
● 6 TBSP SOY SAUCE	● 2 STALKS BOK CHOY, BOTH WHITE AND GREEN PARTS SHREDDED
● 4 TSP 5-SPICE POWDER	
● 1 TSP BLACK PEPPER	
● 1 TSP SUGAR	● 1 LB EGGROLL WRAPPERS
● 1 TBSP CORNSTARCH	● VEGETABLE OIL FOR DEEP-FRYING
● ½ LB GROUND PORK	
● 4 OZ COOKED BABY SHRIMP	● 1 EGG, LIGHTLY BEATEN
● 1 TSP VEGETABLE OIL	**APRICOT SAUCE**
● 8 OZ BEAN SPROUTS	● ½ CUP APRICOT PRESERVES
● 1 CAN (8 OZ) BAMBOO SHOOTS, SHREDDED	● ¼ CUP WHITE WINE VINEGAR
● 1 CAN (8 OZ) WATER CHESTNUTS, SHREDDED	● 1 TSP MINCED GINGERROOT
	● 1 TBSP HONEY

A common eggroll problem is that they usually are served with an overly sweet sauce that overpowers the delicate flavors of the vegetables which give eggrolls their character. Our version is a slightly sour apricot sauce that is gently flavored with fresh ginger. It plays nicely against the slightly spicy flavor of our eggrolls.

1 Soak black mushrooms in cold water for 1 hour or until soft. While they are soaking, combine sesame oil, soy sauce, 5-spice powder, pepper, sugar, and cornstarch. Set aside.

2 In a wok or large skillet, stir-fry the pork, breaking it up into small pieces, until pork is no longer pink. Add shrimp and cook for 1 minute to heat through. Remove to a plate and drain off grease.

3 Cut off tough stems of black mushrooms and discard stems. Shred mushrooms.

4 Heat 1 teaspoon of vegetable oil in the wok or large skillet. Add bean sprouts, bamboo shoots, water chestnuts, scallions, bok choy, and black mushrooms and stir-fry until just heated through. Add pork and shrimp and soy sauce mixture and cook, stirring constantly, until heated through. Set aside to cool.

5 To make sauce, combine apricot preserves, vinegar, ginger, and honey in a small saucepan. Bring to a boil, stirring constantly. Cool before serving. You should have about ⅔ cup.

6 Preheat oil to 375 degrees. Fill one eggroll wrapper at a time. With point of wrapper toward the

cook, place 2 heaping tablespoons of filling in center. Roll eggroll 1 full turn, tuck side corners toward center, and brush them and opposite end of wrapper liberally with beaten egg. Continue rolling until sealed shut. Repeat with remaining filling and wrappers.

7 Deep-fry eggrolls until golden. Serve hot with Slightly Sour Apricot Sauce.

SERVES 10 TO 12

Note
5-spice powder is available in oriental food stores. It is a blend of cloves, cinnamon, fennel seed, Sichuan peppercorns, and star anise.

Fried Cauliflower in a Curried Beer Batter

1 Preheat oil to 375 degrees. Break and separate cauliflower into bite-sized flowerets. Wash and pat dry.

2 Combine flour, baking powder, salt, curry powder, oil, and beer. Dip cauliflower into batter, then deep-fry until golden. This will take about 1 minute. Drain on paper towel. Repeat with remaining cauliflower and batter and serve hot with Mango Chutney.

SERVES 20

● VEGETABLE OIL FOR	● 2 TSP CURRY POWDER
DEEP-FRYING	● 1 TBSP VEGETABLE OIL
● 1 HEAD CAULIFLOWER	● 1 CUP FLAT BEER
● 1 CUP ALL-PURPOSE FLOUR	● MANGO CHUTNEY (PAGE
● 1 TSP BAKING POWDER	191)
● 1 TSP SALT	

Note

Do not prepare batter until just before using. If allowed to stand, it may turn bitter.

Fried Oysters

● 3 CUPS ALL-PURPOSE FLOUR	● ¼ TSP HOT PEPPER SAUCE
● ½ TBSP BAKING POWDER	● 1 EGG, LIGHTLY BEATEN
● 1½ TSP SALT	● 1 CAN (12 OZ) BEER, FLAT
● FRESHLY GROUND WHITE PEPPER	● OIL FOR DEEP-FRYING
	● 36 SHUCKED OYSTERS
● 3 TBSP VEGETABLE OIL	● COCKTAIL SAUCE (PAGE 198)

1 Stir together 2 cups flour, baking powder, salt, and pepper to taste.

2 Stir together 3 tablespoons oil, hot pepper sauce, and egg. Stir into flour mixture. Whisk in beer to make a mixture the consistency of pancake batter. If necessary, add a tablespoon or two of water to thin the batter.

3 In deep-fryer or heavy-bottomed skillet, heat 2 inches oil to 375 degrees. Place remaining cup of flour on a plate. Roll oysters in flour and shake off excess. Dip oysters into batter, letting excess drip off.

4 Fry oysters in hot oil, a few at a time, until golden brown on both sides, about 3 to 5 minutes total. Drain on paper towels. Serve with Cocktail Sauce.

SERVES 12

Note

Keep oysters warm by placing them on a cookie sheet in a 200-degree oven while frying remainder.

133

Calzone

● 1 PACKAGE ACTIVE DRY YEAST	● 4 OZ PROSCIUTTO OR HAM, OR COMBINATION
● ¾ CUP WARM WATER	● ¼ CUP PIMIENTO-STUFFED GREEN OLIVES
● ¼ TSP SUGAR	
● 2 CUPS ALL-PURPOSE FLOUR	● 2 TBSP PEELED, SEEDED, AND MINCED PLUM
● 1 TSP SALT	
● VEGETABLE OIL	TOMATOES (OPTIONAL)

For a robust snack at a small get-together, serve whole, hot Calzone. As part of a buffet table for a large group, slice the Calzone into quarters.

1 Combine yeast, ¼ cup warm water, and sugar in a small bowl and stir. Set aside for 10 minutes, until yeast becomes foamy.

2 Meanwhile, combine 1 cup flour and the salt in a large bowl. Make a well in the center and pour in remaining ½ cup water and 1 tablespoon vegetable oil. Add yeast mixture. Stir in flour from the sides to form a wet dough. Stir briskly with a wooden spoon for a minute.

3 Start adding remaining flour, a tablespoon at a time, until dough reaches a sticky consistency that can be kneaded (from ½ to ¾ cup flour may be added). Turn out onto a floured board, using some of the remaining flour, and knead dough well. When it is smooth and elastic, place in greased bowl, turning to grease all sides. Cover with towel and set aside in warm, draft-free place to rise, about 1 hour.

4 Chop prosciutto or ham with olives and mix with tomatoes if used. In a large, deep skillet, preheat 1 inch of vegetable oil to 375 degrees.

5 Punch dough down on floured board and divide into 12 equal pieces. With floured hands, pat each piece into a circle. Top each circle with the prosciutto mixture. Fold each circle in half and pinch edges well to seal. Each circle will be formed into a crescent about 3½ inches long. Keep crescents on floured board while working with remaining dough.

6 Dust flour off Calzone before lowering into hot oil. Fry several at a time, but don't crowd. Cook for about 2 minutes on one side, or until golden. Then turn over and cook about 2 minutes on the second side. Remove and drain on paper towels. Fry remaining Calzone.

SERVES 12

Note
The Calzone can be prepared in advance and rewarmed in a preheated 325-degree oven for about 10 minutes.

Catfish Fritters

● 1½ LB BONELESS CATFISH	● FRESHLY GROUND WHITE
FILLETS	PEPPER
● 1¾ CUPS MILK	● VEGETABLE OIL FOR
● ¾ CUP SELF-RISING FLOUR	DEEP-FRYING
(SEE NOTE)	● SALT
● ½ CUP CORNMEAL	● COCKTAIL SAUCE (PAGE
● 1 EGG, BEATEN	198)

Deep-fried chunks of sweet catfish can be the surprise hit of this chapter. Each fritter is such a meaty morsel.

1 Cut catfish fillets into 1- to 1½-inch cubes. Place in medium-size bowl. Cover with 1 cup of milk and soak for 30 minutes, then drain.

2 Combine flour and cornmeal in a bowl. Mix together remaining ¾ cup milk and egg. Whisk into flour to make a thick batter. Season with pepper to taste.

3 Heat 1 inch of oil in heavy-bottomed skillet or dutch oven to 375 degrees. Dip fish chunks, a few at a time into batter, allowing excess to drop back into bowl. Ease fritters into hot oil. Allow to cook 3 to 5 minutes on one side, or until golden. Turn over and brown other side. Remove fritters with slotted spoon and place on paper towel-lined cookie sheet.

4 Repeat until all the fish chunks are fried. If desired, place the fish on the cookie sheet in a low oven to keep warm while preparing the remainder. Salt the fritters just before serving and accompany with Cocktail Sauce.

SERVES 10

Note
You can substitute all-purpose flour for the self-rising. Sift together ¾ cup all-purpose flour, 1¼ teaspoons baking powder, and ¾ teaspoon salt.

FAST TAKES

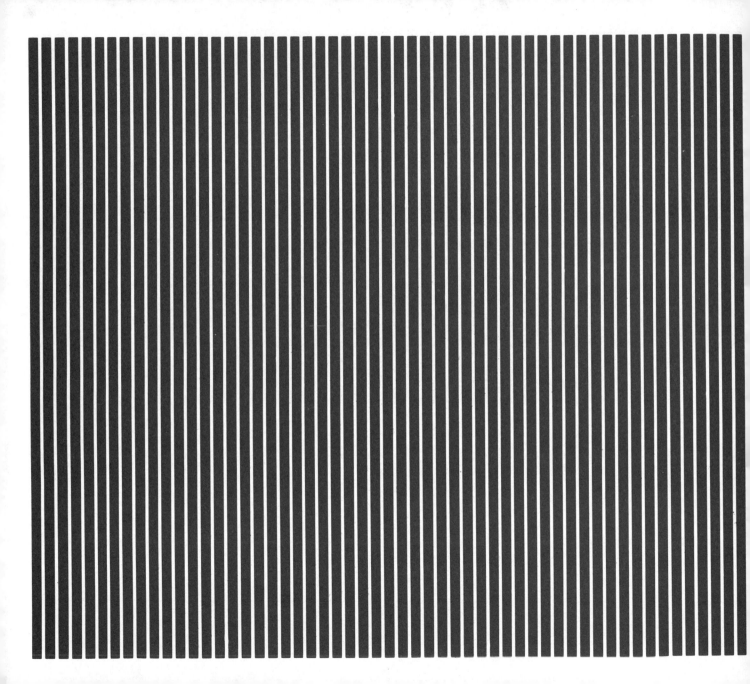

f you know sushi like we know sushi, you'll know why it's included in this chapter on quick dishes. There are three sushi recipes among fourteen items that take only minutes to prepare.

Try Pear Truffles, with that classic combination of pears and gorgonzola all rolled into one, Hummus in Red Pepper Shells, or garlicky Guacamole for instant snacks.

Instead of making Fish Tartare with raw fish that must be finely puréed and sieved, make our version with smoked fish, lemon, and shallots for zesty flavor. Rather than make an intricate vegetable dip, heat together butter, oil, garlic, and anchovies for Bagna Cauda, the best bath a raw mushroom ever had.

You'll think of these foods as the next best thing to having your own caterer in residence.

Opposite: Papaya Draped in Smoked Salmon (recipe on page 149).
Preceding page: Smoked Salmon Sushi (recipe on page 146).

Nuts for Apricots

1 Cream together cream cheese, ginger, and orange marmalade. Spoon into apricots, using about ½ teaspoon filling per apricot. Push an almond into the filling.

2 Cover and chill until serving. If desired, arrange on a small platter and garnish with a circle of slivered almonds.

SERVES 12

● 1 PACKAGE (3 OZ) CREAM	● 2 DOZEN TURKISH DRIED
CHEESE, AT ROOM	APRICOTS
TEMPERATURE	● 24 UNSALTED ALMONDS
● ½ TSP GROUND GINGER	● SLIVERED ALMONDS
● 1½ TBSP ORANGE	(OPTIONAL)
MARMALADE	

Note

Look for apricots that are left whole, except for a small opening to remove the pit. Don't use apricots that are halved.

Guacamole

How are things in guacamole? Just fine.

1 Peel, seed, and mash avocado. Add garlic, red pepper flakes, lemon juice, tomatoes, and salt and pepper to taste.

2 Either serve immediately or place the pit from the avocado in the mixture, cover with plastic wrap, and refrigerate up to 4 hours. (Remove pit before serving.)

MAKES ABOUT 1 CUP

● 1 SOFT, RIPE AVOCADO	● ¼ CUP PEELED, SEEDED,
● 1 CLOVE GARLIC, MINCED	AND CHOPPED FRESH PLUM
¼ TSP CRUSHED RED	TOMATOES
PEPPER FLAKES	● SALT AND PEPPER
● 1 TBSP LEMON JUICE	

Pear Truffles

Pears and gorgonzola cheese are a natural combination. In this concoction, pistachios are added for crunchy texture and a bright green color.

1 Shell pistachio nuts. Rub nuts to remove skins. Chop finely and set aside on a dinner plate.

2 Cream together cheese and 3 tablespoons cream. Mixture should be consistency of firm, spreadable frosting. If necessary, add the fourth tablespoon cream. Set aside.

3 Peel 1 pear. Using a 1-inch melon baller, scoop out 1-inch balls from pear flesh. Work only enough gorgonzola around pear ball to make an even, thin coating. Roll in chopped pistachio nuts and set aside. Repeat with remaining pear balls from first pear. Repeat process with the second pear. Chill several hours, then serve. Do not make more than a day in advance or truffles will become soggy.

SERVES 8 TO 10

● 6 OZ NATURAL (UNDYED) PISTACHIO NUTS	● 3 TO 4 TBSP HEAVY CREAM
● ½ LB GORGONZOLA CHEESE, AT ROOM TEMPERATURE	● 2 LARGE, RIPE PEARS

California Canapés

In the Golden State, the avocado is a staple, used as the basis for a myriad of sandwiches. Bacon, mayonnaise, and curry powder complement it.

1 Place bread on serving platter. Combine mayonnaise and curry powder. Spread on one side of each bread slice.

2 Fry bacon slices in skillet, using bacon press to keep strips flat. While bacon is cooking, peel avocado. Cut lengthwise into 10 slices. When bacon is browned, but not too crisp, quickly pat dry.

3 Work fast so bacon remains pliable. Cut each bacon strip horizontally in 2. Wrap each bacon slice around an avocado slice and place on the piece of bread. Repeat with remaining bacon and avocado slices. Platter looks nice garnished with lemon wedges.

SERVES 10

● 10 SLICES COCKTAIL RYE OR WHOLE WHEAT BREAD	● 5 SLICES BACON
● 3 TBSP MAYONNAISE	● 1 LARGE, RIPE AVOCADO
● ¼ TSP CURRY POWDER	● LEMON WEDGES

Note

If doing in advance, brush each avocado slice lightly with lemon juice. Cover tray tightly with plastic wrap. Refrigerate and bring to room temperature before serving.

Messy Nachos Inspired by Leslee Reis

Let guests build their own appetizers as they mound guacamole and salsa on spicy, cheese-covered taco chips.

1 Preheat oven to 400 degrees. Spread taco chips on a foil-lined cookie sheet.

2 Grate cheese. Toss with jalapeño peppers and coriander. Sprinkle cheese mixture over chips.

3 Bake for 2 minutes or until cheese melts. Watch carefully to avoid burning chips. While piping hot, ease onto serving plate.

4 Serve small bowls of Guacamole and Tomato Salsa with Orange on the side.

SERVES 8 TO 10

• 8 OZ GOOD-QUALITY TACO CHIPS	• 2 TBSP MINCED FRESH CORIANDER (CILANTRO)
• ¾ LB MONTEREY JACK CHEESE	• GUACAMOLE (PAGE 142)
• 5 TO 6 TBSP MINCED, SEEDED JALAPEÑO PEPPERS (ABOUT 4 MEDIUM-SIZE PEPPERS)	• TOMATO SALSA WITH ORANGE (PAGE 197)

Smoked Salmon Sushi

● 1 CUP SUSHI RICE (PAGE	● MINT OR OTHER FRESH
193)	HERB LEAVES
● 1 PIECE (7 BY 8 IN.)	● SOY SAUCE
TOASTED *NORI*	● *WASABI* OR OTHER
● 2 OZ SMOKED SALMON,	HORSERADISH
SLICED THIN	

1 Spread sushi rice in a thin layer over *nori*. Pack down. About 1 inch from the short end, place a line of smoked salmon so that pieces overlap and extend ½ inch beyond ends. Roll up jellyroll fashion.

2 Using a very sharp knife, slice roll into 1-inch pieces. On each piece of sushi, except end pieces which already have salmon protruding, gently pull salmon pieces out so that they extend ½ inch beyond top. Tuck 2 or 3 herb leaves into salmon and serve tepid with soy sauce seasoned to taste with *wasabi* or other horseradish.

SERVES 8

Note

Toasted *nori* is a seaweed and is available, as is *wasabi* horseradish, in oriental food stores.

California Roll Sushi

● 2 CUPS SUSHI RICE (PAGE 193)	● LEMON JUICE
● 1 PIECE (7 BY 8 IN.) TOASTED *NORI*	● SIEVED YOLK OF 1 HARD-COOKED EGG
	● RED CAVIAR
● 1 OZ COOKED CRAB, CUT IN TRIANGULAR STICKS, ABOUT ½ IN. AT WIDEST PART	● SOY SAUCE
	● *WASABI* OR OTHER HORSERADISH
● ¼ OF 1 SMALL AVOCADO, CUT IN TRIANGULAR STICKS, ABOUT ½ IN. AT WIDEST PART	

1 Wet a kitchen towel, squeeze excess moisture out, and place a 1¼-cup layer of sushi rice over it in a 7- by 8-inch rectangle. Top with a layer of toasted *nori*. Press down firmly to pack rice together. Top *nori* with remaining rice, packed down.

2 Place wedges of crab, in a single line, across short end of rice-covered *nori*. Dip avocado in lemon juice. Next to crab, place avocado wedges in a single line. Roll up jellyroll fashion.

3 Using a very sharp knife, slice roll into 1-inch pieces. Sprinkle each piece with sieved egg yolk and red caviar. Serve tepid with soy sauce seasoned to taste with *wasabi* or other horseradish.

SERVES 8

Note
Toasted *nori* is a seaweed and is available, as is *wasabi* horseradish, in oriental food stores.

147

Not So Sushi

Here's the perfect snack for those who love sushi in spirit, but prefer their food slightly more cooked.

1 Press 1 tablespoon sushi rice into an oblong 2 inches by 1 inch. Top with a piece of roast beef that is 3 inches long and 1½ inches wide. Top with a dab of horseradish, and then a pickle fan. (To make pickle fans, slice each cornichon lengthwise, almost to the end in several places. Spread slices to make a fan.) Repeat with remaining ingredients.

2 Serve tepid with soy sauce for dipping.

SERVES 12

● ¾ CUP SUSHI RICE (PAGE 193)	● 1 TBSP *WASABI* OR OTHER HORSERADISH
● 8 OZ LEAN, RARE ROAST BEEF, SLICED ⅛- TO ¼-IN. THICK	● 12 CORNICHON PICKLES
	● SOY SAUCE

Papaya or Melon Draped in Smoked Salmon

Papaya or Melon Draped in Smoked Salmon is so easy to prepare, this introduction is almost as long as the recipe.

1 Remove seeds from papayas or melon; peel, and cut into 24 slices.

2 Drape 1 piece (½ ounce) of smoked salmon over each slice of fruit. Serve cold or tepid with lime wedges so that each slice can be drizzled with lime just before eating.

SERVES 12

● 2 MEDIUM PAPAYAS, OR ½	● 3 LIMES, CUT IN EIGHTS
MEDIUM MELON OF CHOICE	
● 12 OZ SMOKED SALMON,	
SLICED THIN	

Hummus in Red Pepper Shells

● 3 CUPS COOKED CHICKPEAS	● 1 CUP TAHINI
● 4 CLOVES GARLIC, MINCED	● ½ TO 1 TSP SALT
● 1½ CUPS LEMON JUICE	● 5 TO 7 RED BELL PEPPERS

Serve hummus-filled red bell peppers in a cluster on a tray along with pita bread, whole wheat Indian bread, Toasted Bagel Thins (page 67), or Chili Breadsticks (page 119).

1 In a food processor, blender, or with a hand mixer, purée chickpeas. Add garlic, lemon juice, tahini, and salt and mix to combine. Add water, a tablespoon at a time, until hummus is fluffy and of spreading consistency.

2 Cut tops off peppers and remove seeds.

3 Spoon mixture into hollowed-out pepper shells, then place in a cluster on a tray along with an assortment of breads.

SERVES 20

Almost Fish Tartare

Almost Fish Tartare was inspired by steak tartare. Although, literally speaking, the fish is not raw as in the beef version, but has been "cooked" by smoking, the flavors are so natural and pure that it reminds us of the famous steak dish which was its inspiration.

1 Carefully remove any skin and bones from fish fillets. Chop fish in coarse pieces by hand or with food processor. If food processor is used, be careful not to overprocess. By hand, fold in lemon juice, parsley, shallots, and a liberal sprinkling of freshly ground white pepper.

2 Mound into a crock and serve tepid or chilled with sliced pumpernickel bread.

SERVES 6 TO 8

• 1 LB SMOKED FISH FILLETS	• 1 TO 2 SHALLOTS, MINCED
(SELECT ANY OILY FISH	• FRESHLY GROUND WHITE
SUCH AS SABLE)	PEPPER
• 2 TBSP LEMON JUICE	• PUMPERNICKEL BREAD
• 1 TBSP MINCED PARSLEY	

Bagna Cauda

● 12 TBSP UNSALTED BUTTER	● CLEANED AND TRIMMED
● ¼ CUP OLIVE OIL	MUSHROOMS, BROCCOLI
● 8 CLOVES GARLIC, MINCED	FLOWERETS, CAULIFLOWER
● 2 TBSP ANCHOVY PASTE	FLOWERETS, AND GREEN
	PEPPER STRIPS

Serve this pungent, garlicky sauce to a group of friends who aren't faint-hearted. Any leftover sauce can be poured over hot spaghetti for an inexpensive, light entree.

1 In the top of a double boiler, over simmering water, combine butter, olive oil, and garlic. Let butter melt, stirring occasionally. Add anchovy paste and heat through.

2 Transfer mixture to serving dish with attached heat unit. Arrange vegetables around Bagna Cauda, and provide skewers or fondue forks for dipping.

SERVES 6

Note
This mixture can be made up to one hour in advance and kept warm. Do not overheat or it will separate.

Onion Slices

● 10 THIN SLICES WHITE BREAD	● 1 MEDIUM-SIZE RED ONION
● MAYONNAISE	● ½ CUP MINCED FRESH WATERCRESS

1 Using a 2-inch cookie cutter, cut 2 circles out of each bread slice for a total of 20 circles. Spread about ½ teaspoon mayonnaise on 10 circles. Peel onion and slice into 10 paper-thin slices. Place on top of the 10 mayonnaise-covered circles. Cover with remaining bread.

2 Spread a layer of mayonnaise on the rim between the 2 bread slices to cover the opening. Set aside and continue with remaining sandwiches.

3 Place watercress on a flat plate. Roll the mayonnaise-covered edges of each sandwich in the watercress. Gently remove any excess watercress. Place sandwiches on serving platter; cover with plastic wrap and chill 2 to 3 hours before serving.

SERVES 5

Tapenade Tomatoes

● 22 TO 25 CHERRY	● 1 TBSP CHOPPED FRESH
TOMATOES (ABOUT 1 PINT)	BASIL
● ¾ CUP PITTED, IMPORTED	● 1 TBSP CHOPPED FRESH
OIL-CURED OLIVES	PARSLEY
● 4 ANCHOVY FILLETS	● 1 TBSP LEMON JUICE
● 1 CLOVE GARLIC, PEELED	● ¼ CUP OLIVE OIL
● 2 TBSP WELL-DRAINED	● PARSLEY OR LETTUCE
CAPERS	

The world of cooks is divided into those who enjoy stuffing food into food, and those who would rather skip that step. This pungent mixture of olives, anchovies, capers, basil, and garlic can be piled onto a plate and accompanied by bread and vegetables—it's stuff enough.

1 Cut tops off cherry tomatoes. Seed and turn tomatoes upside down on a plate to drain. Coarsely chop olives and set aside. Rinse anchovies in cold water and pat dry.

2 In a blender or food processor fitted with steel blade, combine olives, anchovies, garlic, capers, basil, parsley, and lemon juice. Process until finely minced. Turn food processor or blender on and drizzle in olive oil. Remove mixture to a bowl and stir well.

3 Pack each cherry tomato with about 1½ teaspoons olive mixture. Set on parsley or lettuce-lined plate. Serve tepid.

SERVES 6 TO 10

Note

This can be made several days in advance and refrigerated, but bring to room temperature before serving. Don't freeze and don't fill tomatoes until 1 hour before serving.

Opposite: Tapenade Tomatoes. Following pages: Ratatouille Lemons (recipe on page 159). Steamed Red Snapper (recipe on page 165). Marbled Tea Eggs (recipe on page 168); with Manhattan (recipe on page 21).

FOODS THAT PAN OUT

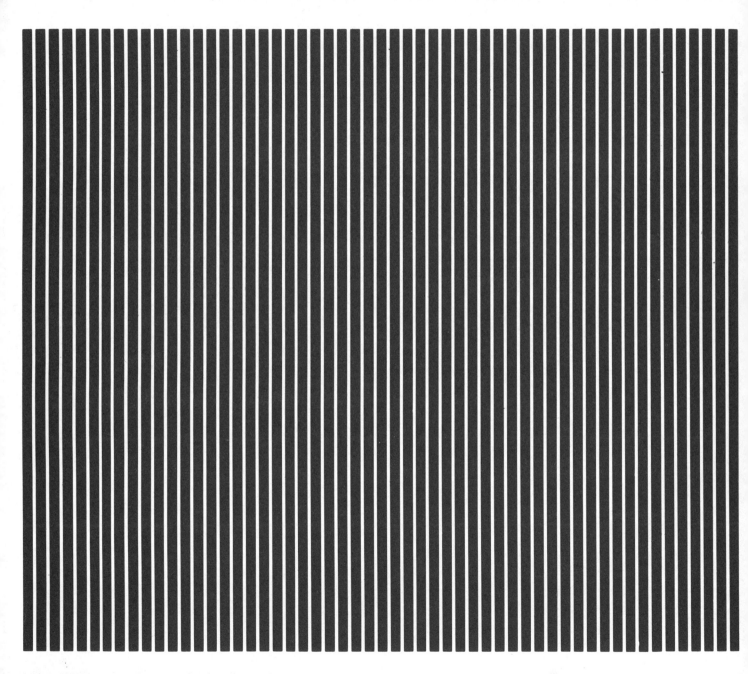

The oven's as full as the summer cottage on the July Fourth weekend, and you've hardly begun to cook. What do you do? Prepare a selection of great stovetop appetizers.

Prepare Ratatouille Lemons, and let them chill in the refrigerator. Make Marbled Tea Eggs with their sepia-lace design, and refrigerate. Make hot and sweet Scallops Remoulade, and chill. The burners are ready for more recipes.

Switch to the warm foods just before guests arrive. A skillet filled with Kashmiri Spiced Meatballs provides an alluring aroma. Onion and Potato Frittata is so tempting it might not make it to the table.

Ratatouille Lemons

● 1 EGGPLANT (1 LB)	● ½ CUP MINCED FRESH
● 1 TBSP KOSHER SALT	PARSLEY
● 1 MEDIUM ONION, PEELED	● ½ CUP MINCED FRESH
AND CHOPPED	BASIL
● OLIVE OIL	● 1 TSP DRIED OREGANO
● 2 CLOVES GARLIC, MINCED	● FRESHLY GROUND BLACK
● 1 RED BELL PEPPER,	PEPPER
CORED, SEEDED, AND	● 2 CUPS CANNED, DRAINED
DICED	TOMATOES
● 1 GREEN BELL PEPPER,	● 18 LEMONS
CORED, SEEDED, AND	
DICED	
● 2 MEDIUM ZUCCHINI OR	
YELLOW SUMMER SQUASH,	
DICED	

1 Don't peel eggplant, but cut into ½-inch cubes. Toss with salt and set aside.

2 Meanwhile, sauté onion in ¼ cup olive oil in large skillet for 5 minutes, until transparent, but not browned. Add garlic and sauté 5 minutes longer. Add peppers, zucchini, and ½ cup more olive oil. Simmer 5 minutes.

3 Press moisture out of eggplant and add to skillet. Add parsley, basil, oregano, and pepper to taste. Seed tomatoes and tear into small chunks. Add to vegetable mixture. Simmer 30 minutes, covered, stirring occasionally. Adjust seasonings. Set aside to cool to tepid, but don't refrigerate.

4 To serve, cut 14 lemons vertically in half, scoop out insides (save for lemonade), and spoon about ¼ cup ratatouille into each lemon cup. Arrange on a platter and garnish with remaining lemons, cut into wedges.

SERVES 28

Note
Ratatouille can be made several days in advance and refrigerated. Bring to room temperature before serving.

Corn Crêpes

1 Beat together eggs, egg yolk, and milk. Stir together salt, flour, and cornmeal and whisk into egg mixture. Add melted butter. Let stand 30 minutes.

2 Lightly coat a 5-inch skillet with clarified butter. Spoon in ½ tablespoon batter and rotate pan to make a crêpe about 3 inches in diameter. Cook about 2 minutes on the first side, turn over, and cook 30 seconds on the second side. Remove to a platter and repeat. Brush pan with more clarified butter as it needs it.

MAKES ABOUT 45 CRÊPES

● 2 EGGS, AT ROOM TEMPERATURE	● ½ TSP SALT
	● ½ CUP ALL-PURPOSE FLOUR
● 1 EGG YOLK, AT ROOM TEMPERATURE	● ½ CUP CORNMEAL
	● 2 TBSP BUTTER, MELTED
● 1 CUP MILK	● 2 TBSP CLARIFIED BUTTER

Note

Use these crêpes to wrap chorizo, guacamole, or sour cream and caviar.

160

Chorizo Fingers

Chorizos are bold, robust sausages that can be served plain, for a gutsy appetizer, or wrapped in a corn crêpe for a more elaborate dish.

1 In meat grinder or food processor fitted with steel blade, grind together pork, beef, pork fat, and garlic. If using a food processor, be sure not to over-process. Remove and discard any gristle.

2 Place meat in a large bowl. Add paprika, oregano, brown sugar, salt, red pepper flakes, hot pepper sauce, *quatre epice,* cinnamon, cumin, and red wine vinegar. Knead by hand to incorporate all seasonings. Cover and refrigerate overnight.

3 Form meat mixture into fingers about 2 inches long and ½ inch in diameter. Heat olive oil in large skillet. Add enough fingers to make a single layer and cook in hot oil, over medium heat, turning to brown all sides, for about 5 minutes. Drain on paper towels.

SERVES 15 TO 25

● 1 LB LEAN BONELESS PORK,	● ½ TSP *QUATRE EPICE*
CUBED	(MIXED PEPPER, NUTMEG,
● ½ LB LEAN BONELESS BEEF,	CLOVES, CINNAMON OR
CUBED	GINGER)
● ¼ LB FRESH PORK FAT,	● ¼ TSP GROUND CINNAMON
CUBED	● ¼ TSP GROUND CUMIN
● 3 CLOVES GARLIC, PEELED	● 2 TBSP RED WINE VINEGAR
● 2 TSP PAPRIKA	● 4 TBSP OLIVE OIL
● ½ TSP DRIED OREGANO	● CORN CRÊPES (PAGE 160)
● 1½ TSP BROWN SUGAR	● MANGO CHUTNEY (PAGE
● ½ TSP SALT OR TO TASTE	191)
● ½ TSP CRUSHED RED	● TOMATO SALSA WITH
PEPPER FLAKES	ORANGE (PAGE 197)
● ¾ TSP HOT PEPPER SAUCE	

Note

To serve, either arrange on a platter with toothpicks and offer Mango Chutney or Tomato Salsa with Orange on the side, or wrap chorizo in Corn Crêpes and offer the chutney and salsa. Chorizo can be made in advance, cooked, and reheated. Place on a cookie sheet, cover loosely with foil, and heat in a preheated 325-degree oven for about 10 minutes.

Chutney Eggs

1 Peel eggs and cut in half lengthwise. Carefully remove yolks to a bowl. Set whites aside.

2 Combine egg yolks with mayonnaise, chutney, ginger, nutmeg, and salt and pepper to taste. Mash ingredients together with back of a fork, then cream until light and fluffy. Spoon into 12 egg white halves.

SERVES 6 TO 10

● 6 HARD-COOKED EGGS	● ⅛ TSP GROUND NUTMEG
● 2½ TO 3 TBSP MAYONNAISE	● DASH *EACH* OF SALT AND
● 1 TBSP GOOD-QUALITY	FRESHLY GROUND WHITE
MINCED FRUIT CHUTNEY	PEPPER
● ¼ TSP GROUND GINGER	

Note
These can be made up to a day in advance. Cover well with plastic wrap and store in the refrigerator.

162

Kashmiri Spiced Meatballs

● 1 TBSP GROUND	● 3 TBSP BUTTER
CORIANDER	● 1 TBSP VEGETABLE OIL
● 2 TSP GROUND CUMIN	● ½ CUP BEEF BROTH
● 2 TSP PAPRIKA	● MANGO CHUTNEY (PAGE
● 5 TSP *GARAM MASALA*	191)
● 1 TSP CRUSHED RED	**YOGURT SAUCE**
PEPPER FLAKES	● 2 CUPS YOGURT
● 1 TSP SUGAR	● 1 TSP GROUND CUMIN
● 1 TSP SALT	● ½ TSP SALT
● 1 TBSP MINCED	● FRESH CORIANDER LEAVES
GINGERROOT	(CILANTRO)
● 1 LB GROUND LAMB	

From the breathtakingly beautiful northern Indian state of Kashmir, these meatballs are highly spiced but not hot. Serve them either in cumin-flavored yogurt sauce or with chutney.

1 Combine coriander, cumin, paprika, *garam masala,* crushed red pepper flakes, sugar, salt, and ginger. Mix in lamb and make meatballs that are 1½ inches in diameter.

2 Over low heat, in large skillet, lightly brown meatballs in butter and oil. Turn off heat and allow to cool slightly. Add beef broth to pan, cover, and simmer gently for 15 minutes or until lamb is cooked to the desired degree of doneness. Serve with toothpicks and Mango Chutney, or serve hot in yogurt sauce.

3 To make yogurt sauce: In another saucepan, over very low heat, combine yogurt, cumin, and salt. Heat but do not boil. Add drained meatballs, sprinkle with coriander leaves, and serve hot.

SERVES 10 TO 15

Note

Garam masala is a blend of spices that could include cardamom, cinnamon, cloves, black pepper, cumin, and coriander. It is available in Indian food stores.

Shrimp Boil

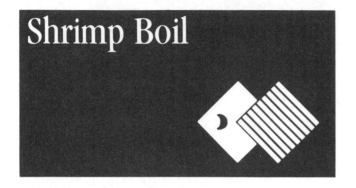

● 2 TBSP CRUSHED RED	● 2 TSP WHOLE CLOVES
PEPPER FLAKES	● 16 OZ (2 CUPS) WHITE
● 3 TBSP DILL SEEDS	WINE
● 2 BAY LEAVES	● 2 LB SHRIMP IN SHELLS
● 1 TSP SALT	● GARLIC-CHILI MAYONNAISE
● 1 TBSP MUSTARD SEEDS	(PAGE 195) OR LEMON
● 1 TSP ALLSPICE BERRIES	WEDGES

This cauldron of bubbling herbs, spices, and wine doesn't alter the flavor of shrimp, but simply enhances its natural sweetness.

1 Bring 2 quarts of water to a boil. Add red pepper flakes, dill seeds, bay leaves, salt, mustard seeds, allspice berries, and whole cloves. Simmer 10 minutes.

2 Add wine and shrimp to pot and bring to a boil. Turn off heat and let stand 8 minutes.

3 Remove shrimp from spice-wine mixture. Serve hot or tepid with Garlic Chili Mayonnaise or lemon wedges.

SERVES 6 TO 8

Note
If desired, shell shrimp and allow to steep 5 minutes before removing from spice-wine mixture.

Steamed Red Snapper

1 Rinse fish with cold water and pat dry. With a sharp knife, make 4 slits on each side of fish. Slits should touch bones but not cut through.

2 Sprinkle 3 tablespoons ginger and half the garlic evenly over inside of fish. Season liberally with black pepper. Place fish in shallow dish that will fit inside steamer. Drizzle with oil and sprinkle with remaining ginger and garlic and season liberally with pepper.

3 Place dish over simmering water, cover tightly, and steam for 20 minutes or until flesh is no longer translucent. Place on serving plate and sprinkle with scallions just before serving. Serve hot, tepid, or cold with cocktail rye bread and fresh lemon wedges or Garlic-Chili Mayonnaise.

SERVES 6 TO 8

• 1 RED SNAPPER, ABOUT 3	• 3 TBSP PEANUT OIL
LB, INSIDES REMOVED BUT	• 4 SCALLIONS, BOTH WHITE
HEAD AND TAIL LEFT ON	AND GREEN PARTS
(CAN REMOVE HEAD, IF	SHREDDED
DESIRED)	• COCKTAIL RYE BREAD AND
• 6 TBSP MINCED	FRESH LEMON WEDGES OR
GINGERROOT	GARLIC-CHILI MAYONNAISE
• 6 CLOVES GARLIC, MINCED	(PAGE 195)
• FRESHLY GROUND BLACK	
PEPPER	

Steamed Chinese Dumplings

● 10 OZ GROUND PORK	● ½ TO ¾ TSP SALT
● 2 SCALLIONS, BOTH WHITE	● ¼ TSP BLACK PEPPER
AND GREEN PARTS MINCED	● ½ TSP SUGAR
● 2 TBSP MINCED	● 2 TBSP CORNSTARCH
GINGERROOT	● 24 CIRCULAR (3 IN.)
● 1 TBSP SOY SAUCE	WONTON WRAPPERS
● 1 TSP SESAME OIL	● 24 FRESH OR FROZEN PEAS

If served hot off the stove in a Chinese bamboo steamer, these tiny dumplings never fail to amaze eating audiences. As a bonus, the ginger-pepper flavor is delicious.

1 Combine pork, scallions, ginger, soy sauce, sesame oil, salt, pepper, sugar, and cornstarch.

2 Place a heaping teaspoon of filling in the center of a wonton wrapper. Press 4 sides of wrapper into filling to make a cup. Press 4 protruding corners of the wrapper into filling so that filling is packed tightly and dough looks pleated around the top.

3 Press 1 pea into the top of the filling. Repeat with remaining filling and wonton wrappers.

4 Oil a steamer and place dumplings over simmering water. Cover and steam for 30 minutes or until centers of dumplings are no longer pink. Serve hot in a bamboo steamer.

SERVES 12

Note

Round wonton wrappers usually are called *gyoza* wrappers. If they are not available, substitute wonton wrappers and cut them into circles.

Onion and Potato Frittata

• ¾ CUP POTATOES, PEELED	• 6 EGGS, LIGHTLY BEATEN
AND SLICED ¼ IN. THICK,	• SALT AND BLACK PEPPER
1½ IN. WIDE	• 1¼ CUPS GRATED
• 3 CUPS SLICED YELLOW	PARMESAN CHEESE
ONIONS	• GREENS
• 5 TBSP OLIVE OIL	
• 4 CLOVES GARLIC, MINCED	

Straight from the Spanish snack tradition called *tapas,* but with a detour through Italy for Parmesan cheese, this frittata proves eggs aren't just for breakfast anymore.

1 In a 9-inch nonstick frying pan, sauté potatoes and onions in olive oil until potatoes are tender. Add garlic and sauté for 1 minute. Do not allow garlic to brown.

2 Pour in beaten eggs, season to taste with salt and pepper, and sprinkle evenly with cheese. Cook frittata over low heat until eggs are firm on top.

3 Cover the pan with a plate and invert both frying pan and plate. Gently slide frittata from plate back into frying pan. Place pan back over medium heat for a few minutes so that bottom of frittata lightly browns. Serve frittata hot, tepid, or cold on a bed of greens.

SERVES 6 TO 8

Note
Sliced bell peppers, 1 green and 1 red, can be substituted for onion in this frittata.

Marbled Tea Eggs

● 12 EGGS	● 4 TSP LOOSE TEA
● 2 TBSP SALT	● SOY SAUCE
● 3 TBSP SOY SAUCE	● MINCED CHIVES
● 2 WHOLE STAR ANISE	

Beautiful Marbled Tea Eggs have a slightly smokey flavor that goes well with fowl.

1 Place eggs in saucepan. Cover with water. Bring to a boil, turn down heat very low, and simmer gently for 10 minutes. Remove from heat. Pour out hot water. Add just enough cold water to cover. Pick up each egg and tap it gently with the back of a spoon to cause tiny cracks.

2 Return eggs to water. Add salt, soy sauce, star anise, and tea to water. Stir gently to mix. Bring to a boil. Turn down heat very low, cover, and simmer for 2 hours. Check every 30 minutes to make sure water has not boiled away. If water level dips below top of eggs, add more hot water.

3 Refrigerate eggs in tea brine at least 8 hours. Before serving, remove shells and slice eggs in half. Arrange eggs, yolk side down, in concentric circles on a plate with a small bowl of soy sauce sprinkled with minced chives in the center for dipping. Serve cold or tepid.

SERVES 12

Note
Star anise is available at oriental food stores.

New Potatoes Tonnato

New Potatoes Tonnato is a hearty dish that is the perfect partner to dark beer. Arranged on a platter with Tapenade Tomatoes, Potatoes Tonnato makes a visually interesting as well as full-flavored hors d'oeuvre.

1 Wash potatoes and steam until tender, about 30 minutes. Cool. While potatoes are cooling, combine olive oil, egg yolk, lemon juice, cayenne pepper, and anchovy fillets. Mix in blender, food processor, or with hand mixer until thoroughly combined. By hand fold in tuna and capers.

2 Slice potatoes in half, trim bottoms a bit so that potato halves sit flat, scoop out a bit of the center, and top with tuna mixture. Sprinkle each potato with parsley and serve tepid surrounded with Tapenade Tomatoes.

SERVES ABOUT 10

● 10 SMALL NEW POTATOES	● 1 CAN (6½ OZ) TUNA IN
● ¼ CUP OLIVE OIL	OIL, DRAINED
● 1 EGG YOLK	● 1 TABLESPOON DRAINED
● 1 TBSP LEMON JUICE	CAPERS
● ⅛ TO ¼ TSP CAYENNE	● ¼ CUP MINCED PARSLEY
PEPPER	● TAPENADE TOMATOES
● 2 ANCHOVY FILLETS,	(PAGE 154)
MASHED TO A PULP	

Baby Eggplant under Ripe Olives and Red Peppers

1 Steam whole baby eggplants and red pepper until tender, about 2 minutes for pepper and 5 minutes for eggplant. Cool.

2 Halve eggplants lengthwise, leaving end on. Scoop out a few of the seeds but leave most of the pulp. Discard seeds. Sprinkle eggplant halves with lemon juice.

3 Over low heat, sauté garlic in olive oil and butter for a minute. Add tomato sauce and tomato paste. Stir in olives and peppers and season to taste with salt and freshly ground pepper. Mound filling onto baby eggplant halves and serve tepid on a bed of greens.

SERVES 10 TO 12

● 8 BABY EGGPLANTS	● 2 TBSP TOMATO SAUCE
● 1 RED BELL PEPPER, CUT IN ½-IN. DICE	● 2 TBSP TOMATO PASTE
● JUICE OF ½ LEMON	● ⅔ CUP SLICED RIPE OLIVES
● 5 GARLIC CLOVES, MINCED	● SALT AND FRESHLY GROUND BLACK PEPPER
● 1 TBSP OLIVE OIL	● GREENS
● 1 TBSP BUTTER	

Opposite: California Roll Sushi (recipe on page 147).

Garlicky Shrimp

Save this recipe for friends who love to get down and have a messy good time with food. Set out little bowls for the shrimp shells, plenty of napkins, crusty Whole Wheat French Bread (page 120) for dunking, and lots of beer.

1 Melt butter in dutch oven. Remove from heat. Add oil, garlic, bay leaves, oregano, salt and pepper to taste, crushed red pepper flakes, lemon juice, and shrimp. Toss well. Set aside for 30 minutes (butter may solidify), stirring occasionally.

2 Place over low to medium heat and allow to come to a bubble gently, not vigorously. Stir. Cover and cook shrimp 5 minutes or just until they turn bright pink. Pour shrimp into a ceramic bowl that will keep them hot and bring to the table. Guests can dig in with their fingers or with long forks.

SERVES 6

½ CUP BUTTER	1 TSP CRUSHED RED
¼ CUP VEGETABLE OIL	PEPPER FLAKES
2 CLOVES GARLIC, MINCED	DASH OF LEMON JUICE
2 BAY LEAVES	1 LB MEDIUM TO LARGE
½ TSP DRIED OREGANO,	SHRIMP IN THE SHELL
CRUSHED	
SALT AND FRESHLY GROUND	
BLACK PEPPER TO TASTE	

Note

This recipe can easily be doubled or tripled, but don't crowd the shrimp mixture in the cooking pot. Also be sure to use a dish that keeps the shrimp hot or warm; otherwise shrimp will taste greasy.

Opposite: Daiquiri (recipe on page 22).

Sea Scallop Escabeche with Sichuan Peppercorns

● 1½ LB SEA SCALLOPS	● 4 DRIED CHILI PEPPERS
● ¾ CUP ALL-PURPOSE FLOUR	● 2 BAY LEAVES
● ½ CUP OLIVE OIL	● 1 TSP SICHUAN
● 3 CARROTS, SLICED	PEPPERCORNS
DIAGONALLY	● ½ TSP 5-SPICE POWDER
● 5 CLOVES GARLIC, PEELED	● ½ TSP SALT
AND SLIGHTLY CRUSHED	● 8 OZ (1 CUP) SAKE
● 1 MEDIUM-SIZED ONION,	
PEELED AND SLICED	

This dish blends fresh seafood with spices from China and sake from Japan. Exotic seasonings give it a slightly hot background flavor, even though it is to be served tepid.

1 Place sea scallops in a bag with flour and shake until scallops are lightly dusted. Shake off excess flour. In a large skillet, heat ¼ cup olive oil until very hot. Add scallops and stir-fry until they just turn golden. This will take 1 to 2 minutes. Remove from skillet.

2 Add remaining ¼ cup olive oil to skillet and stir-fry carrots, garlic, and onion over high heat for 2 minutes. Add chili peppers, bay leaves, Sichuan peppercorns, 5-spice powder, salt, and sake. Cover and simmer for 10 minutes.

3 Pour mixture in skillet over scallops, cover tightly, and refrigerate for 24 hours. Stir several times to combine. Serve tepid with toothpicks.

SERVES 8 TO 10

Note

Five-spice powder is available in oriental food stores. It is a blend of cloves, cinnamon, fennel seed, Sichuan peppercorns, and star anise.

Steamed Mussels with Mustard Sauce

● 2 LB MUSSELS	● 1 EGG YOLK
● 8 OZ (1 CUP) DRY VERMOUTH	● 2 TBSP PREPARED DIJON-STYLE MUSTARD
● ½ CUP WATER	● 1 TSP SUGAR
● 1 SHALLOT, COARSELY CHOPPED	● FRESHLY GROUND WHITE PEPPER
● 2 BAY LEAVES	● 1 TBSP MINCED SCALLIONS, GREEN PART ONLY
● ½ CUP SOUR CREAM	

1 Scrub mussels, removing beards with a sharp tug to the shell. Discard any open mussels.

2 In a large pot, bring to a boil the vermouth, water, shallot, and bay leaves. Add the mussels, cover the pot, and steam for about 3 to 5 minutes, or until the shells open. Shake the pot occasionally. Set aside to cool. Discard any mussels that don't open.

3 Remove top halves of shells and discard. Set mussels with their bottom shells on serving platter.

4 In a bowl, combine sour cream, egg yolk, mustard, sugar, and white pepper to taste. Fold in scallions. Top each mussel with about ½ teaspoon sauce. Serve cold.

SERVES 10

Note

Mussels and sauce can be made up to 4 hours in advance and stored, well-wrapped in the refrigerator. Don't assemble the dish until the last minute. The mussels and cream are delicate and should not sit for hours on a buffet table in a warm room.

Scallops in Remoulade Sauce

● ½ CUP MAYONNAISE	● ⅛ TSP HOT PEPPER SAUCE
● 1 TSP DIJON-STYLE	● ¼ TSP GOOD-QUALITY
MUSTARD	PAPRIKA
● DASH OF LEMON JUICE	● 8 OZ (1 CUP) DRY WHITE
● 1 SMALL CLOVE GARLIC,	WINE
MINCED	● 2 BAY LEAVES
● ½ TBSP DRAINED SMALL	● ½ LB FRESH BAY SCALLOPS
CAPERS	
● 1 TSP CRUSHED DRIED	
TARRAGON	

Sometimes it's a cozy change to just invite a few friends over for cocktails and appetizers. Then a recipe like the Scallops in Remoulade Sauce, which makes four servings, is appropriate. Considering how sensational it tastes, it might be a good idea to double the recipe, regardless of the small number of guests.

1 Prepare remoulade sauce by combining mayonnaise, mustard, and lemon juice in a medium bowl. Stir in garlic, capers, tarragon, hot pepper sauce, and paprika. Chill, covered, for at least 1 hour.

2 Bring wine and bay leaves to the boil in a non-aluminum saucepan. Add the bay scallops. Cover the saucepan and shake. Count to 60, while allowing scallops to cook over medium heat. Drain scallops. Discard wine and bay leaves.

3 Chill scallops until cool, then fold into sauce. Chill 2 to 3 hours before serving. Serve with toothpicks or on small cocktail plates.

SERVES 4

174

Crab Cakes

● 3 TBSP BUTTER	● ½ TSP HOT PEPPER SAUCE
● 1 SHALLOT, MINCED	● ¼ TSP DRY MUSTARD
● ½ LB CRABMEAT,	● 1 TBSP MINCED FRESH
PREFERABLY FRESH	PARSLEY
● 1 EGG, BEATEN	● 1 TO 3 TBSP BREAD
● ½ TSP LEMON JUICE	CRUMBS
● SALT AND FRESHLY GROUND	● FLOUR
WHITE PEPPER	● 1 TBSP VEGETABLE OIL

1 Melt 1 tablespoon butter in medium skillet. Add shallot and sauté over low heat until tender, about 5 minutes.

2 Gently press excess liquid from crabmeat and separate crab into small pieces in a bowl. Add shallot, egg, lemon juice, salt and pepper to taste, hot pepper sauce, mustard, and parsley. Add enough bread crumbs to make a mixture that sticks together. Form into small cakes about 1 inch in diameter. Dust with flour on both sides and set aside while preparing remaining cakes.

3 Heat remaining 2 tablespoons butter with oil in skillet. Sauté crab cakes, a few at a time, until lightly browned on both sides, about 5 minutes total. Serve hot.

SERVES 8 TO 10

Note

To keep crab cakes hot, place cooked ones on a cookie sheet in a 200-degree oven while cooking the remainder. These can be rewarmed in preheated 300-degree oven for about 10 minutes.

Chicken with Curry Sauce in Whole Wheat Puffs

This versatile chicken salad can go into Whole Wheat Puffs, avocado halves, melon halves, or even pita bread. It has a fresh, sharp flavor that guests will love.

1 Remove chicken from bones. Discard skin. Cut or tear meat into bite-sized pieces and set aside in bowl. Dice green pepper and add to chicken.

2 Combine mayonnaise, tomato paste, paprika, curry powder, and salt and pepper to taste. Spoon into chicken and peppers, and fold in well. Chill several hours.

3 Fill puffs just before serving. Serve cold.

SERVES 18 TO 20

● 4 CHICKEN BREAST HALVES,	● ⅛ TSP PAPRIKA
COOKED IN CHICKEN BROTH	● A ROUNDED ½ TEASPOON
AND ALLOWED TO COOL	CURRY POWDER
● ½ MEDIUM-SIZED GREEN	● SALT AND WHITE PEPPER
BELL PEPPER	● WHOLE WHEAT PUFFS
● ⅔ CUP MAYONNAISE	(PAGE 199)
● ½ TBSP TOMATO PASTE	

Note

Chicken mixture can be made a day in advance and kept refrigerated.

Scrambled Mushrooms

● 1 LB LARGE MUSHROOMS	● 1 LARGE CLOVE GARLIC,
● 3 TBSP BUTTER	MINCED
● 3 TBSP VEGETABLE OIL	● 2 EGGS
● ¼ CUP FINELY MINCED RED	● ⅛ TSP DRIED THYME
OR GREEN BELL PEPPER, OR	● SALT AND FRESHLY GROUND
A COMBINATION OF BOTH	WHITE PEPPER
● ¼ CUP MINCED ONION	

1 Remove stems from mushrooms (save for another use). Heat together 2 tablespoons butter and 2 tablespoons oil in a large skillet. Add mushroom caps, cavity-side up, and cook about 5 minutes over medium heat. Remove from heat. Discard any liquid that gathered in the caps. Set mushrooms on a cookie sheet and place in a 200-degree oven just to keep warm.

2 To the fat remaining from cooking the mushrooms, add the remaining tablespoon oil. Add the pepper, onion, and garlic, and sauté 5 minutes. Set aside.

3 In a second skillet, melt remaining 1 tablespoon butter. Beat together eggs, thyme, salt, and pepper to taste. Pour into skillet. Add sautéed vegetables. Using a fork, begin to scramble the eggs and vegetables, while cooking over medium heat. Cook just until the eggs are set, but still creamy, 3 to 5 minutes.

4 Remove from heat. Remove the mushrooms from the oven. Fill each mushroom cap with a rounded teaspoonful of egg mixture. It may be necessary to salt the mushrooms lightly before filling. Place on serving tray. Serve hot or tepid.

SERVES 10

Chicken Liver Pâté

● 12 TBSP BUTTER, AT ROOM TEMPERATURE	● ¼ TSP DRIED OREGANO
	● ½ TSP SALT
● 1½ LB CHICKEN LIVERS, TRIMMED OF ALL MEMBRANES AND FAT, AND PATTED DRY	● FRESHLY GROUND BLACK PEPPER
	● ½ CUP HEAVY CREAM, WHIPPED (OPTIONAL)
● 1 CUP THINLY SLICED ONIONS	● BRAIDED WHOLE WHEAT MOLASSES BREAD (PAGE
● 1 CLOVE GARLIC, PEELED AND CRUSHED	118) OR CRACKERS
● ⅛ TSP CRUSHED DRIED SAGE	

1 Melt 4 tablespoons butter in a large, heavy skillet. Sauté chicken livers, about one-third at a time, over medium heat. Cook 3 to 4 minutes on one side, turn over, and cook about 2 minutes on second side. Set aside to cool.

2 When livers are cooked, sauté onions and garlic in same skillet about 5 minutes, until tender. Cool.

3 Pour off any accumulated liquid from the livers. In a blender or food processor fitted with steel blade, combine livers, onions, garlic, sage, oregano, salt, and pepper to taste.

4 For a very smooth pâté, remove liver mixture from food processor or blender and press through a sieve to remove fibers. If omitting this step, just remove the liver mixture and stir to make sure the ingredients are well combined.

5 Cut remaining 8 tablespoons butter into small chunks. Spoon a little of the chicken liver mixture into the food processor or blender. Turn on. Add a few butter chunks and keep machine running until butter is incorporated. Alternately add liver mixture and butter to the machine. Do this as fast as possible, so butter doesn't melt and separate out. (If mixture begins to look a little sad, with butter floating outside the chicken livers, place the mixture, bowl and all, in the refrigerator for 1 hour.)

6 When all the chicken liver mixture and butter have been used, remove the mixture from the food processor or blender. For a light pâté, fold the

whipped cream into the liver; otherwise the mixture will be dense and creamy.

7 Spoon into an attractive 3-cup mold (4-cup mold if using the cream). Chill for several hours. Serve cold with bread or crackers.

SERVES 12

LITTLE BITES

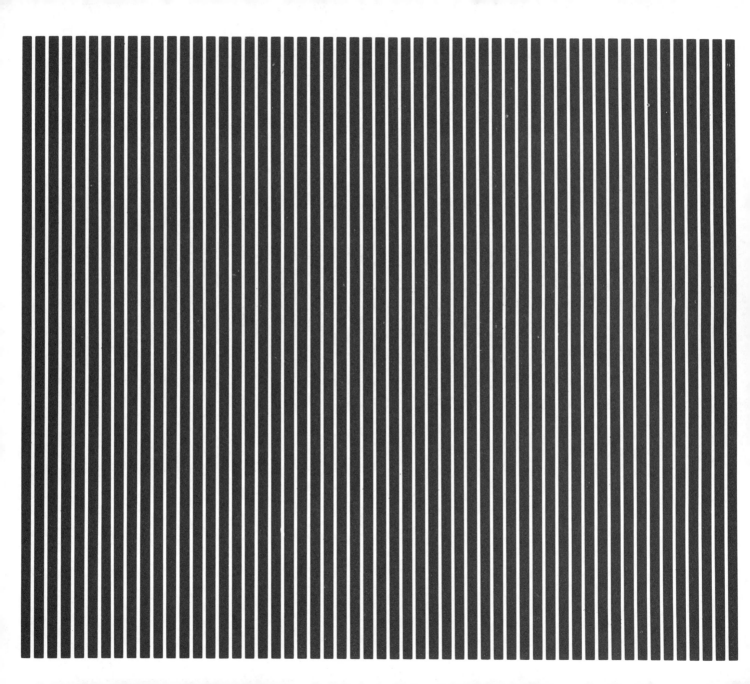

I f you're the kind of person who shares a recipe and then says, "Well, you can also add . . ." or "You can substitute . . ." or "I'll bet if you did . . . with the dish it would be even better," you'll appreciate the following pages.

They are filled with appetizing ideas to think about, expand upon, and make your own. We'll give you the basic concept, the rest is up to you. It's your chapter.

Take salami slices (about 2 to 3 inches in diameter) and form into cones using a toothpick to secure. Dab a little softened cream cheese on the open end of each cone. Press a green or red grape into the cream cheese to resemble a scoop of ice cream in a salami cone.

Mash canned, smoked oysters to a paste and spread on small rounds of Melba toast.

Make crisp little sandwiches by spreading Liptaur cheese (page 57) between two thin slices of peeled cucumber or zucchini. Dust the rim of the sandwiches with paprika.

Toast thin French bread slices, then rub with a garlic clove half and drizzle with olive oil. Serve warm with some gutsy red wine.

Make marinated vegetable kabobs. Buy marinated mushroom caps (or make your own) and pickled onions. Alternate the two with pieces of pimiento on wooden skewers.

Marinate canned and drained artichoke hearts in commercially prepared Italian dressing for an hour. Sprinkle with grated Parmesan cheese before serving. Set out with toothpicks or cocktail forks.

Mash goat cheese with a little heavy cream to a soft, smooth consistency. Dab on the ends of endive leaves.

In a blender or food processor, combine a 4-ounce can of cooked shrimp (drained) with ½ cup cold butter and a few dashes of cayenne pepper. Process just to a smooth paste. Spread shrimp butter on whole wheat toast points and top each with a coriander sprig.

Marinate cooked shrimp or scallops in a vinaigrette spiced with sliced green chilies and finely chopped garlic. Serve with toothpicks.

Line a large bowl with fried corn tortillas. Fill with cooked, ground beef, sliced black olives, chopped green or red bell pepper, canned (drained) kidney beans, chopped onion, and shredded Cheddar cheese. Toss with commercially prepared barbecue sauce to make a moist, but not wet mixture. Serve with additional fried corn tortillas on the side for scooping up the meat mixture.

Serve skewers of fresh fruit with a sauce made by blending 8 ounces of cream cheese, ¼ cup chopped hazelnuts, and honey to taste.

Sprinkle a corn tortilla liberally with Monterey Jack cheese; top with another corn tortilla spread with red salsa. Top with a third corn tortilla sprinkled liberally with shredded Cheddar cheese. Top with a fourth corn tortilla and bake in a preheated 350-degree oven until the cheese melts. Spread with Guacamole (page 142) and top with sour cream. Sprinkle with sliced, canned chilies. Slice into wedges and serve.

Blend softened cream cheese with blue cheese to taste. Use to cover seeded red or seedless green grapes. Roll in chopped pistachios to cover. Chill, then serve.

Prepare small pasta shells, preferably colored ones; cool and fill with Herbed Cheese (page 196). Sprinkle minced parsley over each shell and set out on a parsley-lined platter.

Steam small, tender brussels sprouts. Cool and hollow out a generous cavity from the bottom of each. Fill with commercially prepared or homemade deviled ham.

Splurge on smoked turkey or smoked pheasant (available at many gourmet shops). Slice paper thin and arrange on a plate with figs. Roll slices around figs to eat.

BACK TO BASICS

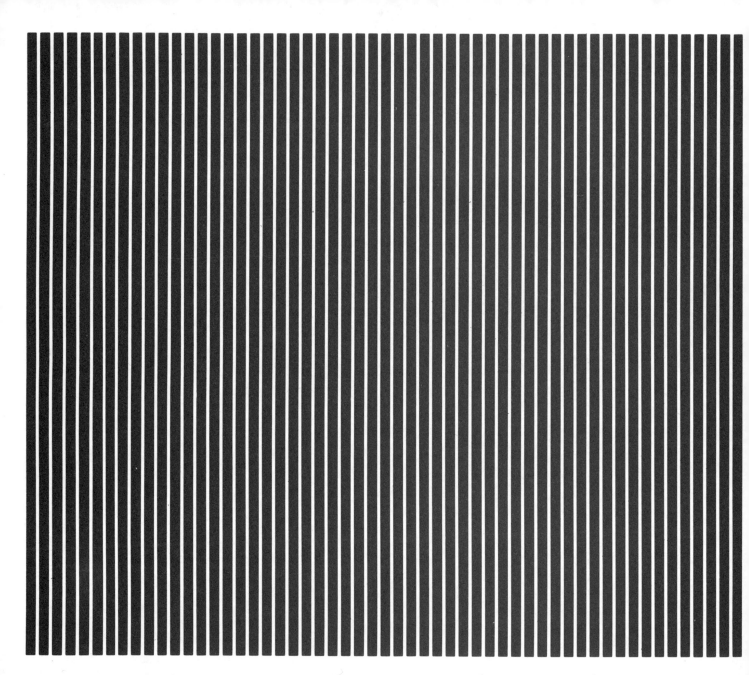

e call these recipes basic because they're as essential to party cooking as club soda is to bartending.

These are the elements that will ensure your success as a cook. You'll appreciate the versatility of the butters, sauces, and doughs. What peace of mind to know that all the little details are worked out.

Our pie crust is failproof; it rolls out without a snag, every time.

Hot Anchovy Butter, Garlic-Parsley Butter, and Orange Honey Butter make simple spreads for our breads, or can replace sauces on grilled fish or chicken.

Mango Chutney, a traditional condiment for Indian food, makes plain cold cuts dazzling as well.

Use Garlic-Chili Mayonnaise for vegetables, shrimp, fish, or chicken salad and you'll never again be tempted to open a jar of sandwich spread.

Garlic-Parsley Butter

This is not a subtle garlic dish, but then, who wants just a hint of garlic? It's marvelous with cornbread or whole wheat bread.

1 Allow butter to soften. Meanwhile place garlic on a small plate and mash with salt to make a paste. Cream together butter, mashed garlic and salt, parsley, and lemon juice.

2 Spoon mixture into butter molds or place on a sheet of plastic wrap and form into a loaf or cylinder. Refrigerate until firm.

MAKES ABOUT ½ CUP

● ½ CUP BUTTER	● 2 TBSP MINCED FRESH
● 1 CLOVE GARLIC, PEELED	PARSLEY
● ⅛ TSP SALT	● DASH OF LEMON JUICE

Hot Anchovy Butter

Use this hot and salty butter to give life to an assortment of otherwise plain breads or crackers.

1 Cream together butter, anchovy paste, and red pepper flakes.

2 Spoon into butter mold or place on a sheet of plastic wrap and form into a loaf or cylinder. Refrigerate until firm.

MAKES ABOUT ½ CUP

● ½ CUP BUTTER, AT ROOM TEMPERATURE	● ½ TSP CRUSHED RED PEPPER FLAKES
● 1 TBSP ANCHOVY PASTE	

Mango Chutney

This may replace ketchup as the standard condiment. It's sweet with an undercurrent of fire that takes the breath away. This chutney can also be put up in jars and will make a welcome gift during the holiday season.

1 Combine mangos, ginger, garlic, onion, jalapeño peppers, mustard seeds, brown sugar, cider vinegar, and salt to taste in heavy-bottomed saucepan.

2 Cover and simmer 2 hours, stirring occasionally, or until mixture is thick.

MAKES ABOUT 3½ CUPS

● 3 CUPS MINCED MANGOS	● 1 TSP MUSTARD SEEDS
(3 RIPE MANGOS)	● 1 CUP FIRMLY PACKED
● 3 TBSP MINCED	BROWN SUGAR
GINGERROOT	● 1 CUP CIDER VINEGAR
● 1 CLOVE GARLIC, MINCED	● SALT
● 1 SMALL ONION, PEELED	
AND MINCED	
● 2 MEDIUM-SIZE JALAPEÑO	
PEPPERS, SEEDED AND	
MINCED	

Note
This can be made several days in advance and refrigerated.

Pastry Crust

1 Mix together flour and salt in a bowl. Cut in butter and shortening with a pastry blender until mixture resembles coarse meal. Whisk together egg yolk and 2 tablespoons water. Pour over flour mixture and stir until pastry comes together. If necessary add part or all of remaining water.

2 Knead dough 2 or 3 times to gather into a ball. Wrap in plastic wrap and chill 30 minutes before using.

MAKES DOUGH FOR 24 MINI-TARTS OR 1 GENEROUS 9-INCH TART

● 1 CUP ALL-PURPOSE FLOUR	● 2 TBSP VEGETABLE
● DASH OF SALT	SHORTENING
● 4 TBSP COLD, UNSALTED	● 1 EGG YOLK
BUTTER, CUT IN SMALL	● 2 TO 3 TBSP WATER
PIECES	

Sushi Rice

1 Combine rice and water. Bring to a boil, turn down heat to the lowest setting, cover, and cook rice until all liquid is absorbed.

2 While rice is cooking, combine vinegar, sugar, and salt, if using, in a saucepan over low heat. Bring to a boil, stirring constantly. When sugar is dissolved, remove from heat.

3 Stir vinegar mixture into hot rice and let sit until liquid is absorbed.

MAKES 2 CUPS

● ¾ CUP SHORT-GRAIN RICE	● 2 TBSP SUGAR
● 1 CUP WATER	● PINCH OF SALT (OPTIONAL)
● 3 TBSP DISTILLED WHITE VINEGAR	

Orange Honey Butter

1 In a food processor, blender, or with hand mixer, mix butter, honey, and orange zest until fluffy.

2 Pack mixture into a serving crock and refrigerate until 30 minutes before serving.

MAKES 1 CUP

● 1 CUP BUTTER, SOFTENED	● GRATED ZEST OF 1 ORANGE
● 4 TSP HONEY	

Garlic-Chili Mayonnaise

This rich mayonnaise takes only minutes to make, is highly flavored, and enhances any steamed or poached seafood. It also is good spread on any sandwich.

1 In a blender or food processor, whirl garlic and chili (use half if only a slightly spicy flavor is desired) until minced. Add egg, egg yolk, salt, and lemon juice and blend until fluffy (about 30 seconds).

2 With machine running, add oils in a very slow, thin stream until all oil is added. This should take several minutes. Serve cold.

MAKES ABOUT 1 CUP

● 3 LARGE CLOVES GARLIC	● 1 EGG YOLK, AT ROOM
● 1 SMALL YELLOW CHILI	TEMPERATURE
PEPPER, SEEDS REMOVED	● ¼ TSP SALT
(OR USE ONLY HALF)	● 1 TBSP LEMON JUICE
● 1 WHOLE EGG, AT ROOM	● ½ CUP CORN OIL
TEMPERATURE	● ½ CUP OLIVE OIL

Herbed Cheese

Here's an easy way to make the higher-priced spread.

1 With an electric mixer, blender, or food processor, whip together garlic, butter, cream cheese, and white wine vinegar. By hand stir in parsley. Refrigerate at least 1 hour or until serving.

2 Serve cold or tepid as a spread for bread. Form into a cylinder and roll in pepper or minced chives and serve with crackers, or double recipe and use as filling in Scallops in Pea-Pod Beds (page 58).

MAKES ⅔ CUP

● 1 SMALL CLOVE GARLIC, MINCED	● 2 TSP MINCED FRESH PARSLEY
● ¼ CUP BUTTER, SOFTENED	● COARSELY GROUND BLACK PEPPER OR MINCED CHIVES
● 3 OZ CREAM CHEESE, SOFTENED	
● 2 TSP TARRAGON WHITE WINE VINEGAR	

Tomato Salsa with Orange

The spiciness of this highly flavored salsa depends upon the heat of the chilies. Those with tender tongues probably would do better to seed the chilies before adding them to the salsa.

1 Combine scallion, onion, coriander, chilies, salt, sugar, orange zest, tomatoes, and juice. Add hot pepper sauce to taste.

2 Chill for at least 2 hours. Serve as a dip with Messy Nachos (page 145). Serve cold.

MAKES ABOUT 2¾ CUPS

● 1 SCALLION, BOTH WHITE AND GREEN PARTS SLICED	● ½ TSP SALT
● ¼ CUP CHOPPED ONION	● ½ TSP SUGAR
● 2 TBSP MINCED FRESH CORIANDER (CILANTRO)	● GRATED ZEST OF 1 ORANGE
● 2 SERRANO OR JALAPEÑO CHILIES (OR TO TASTE), FINELY MINCED	● 1 CAN (16 OZ) TOMATOES, CHOPPED WITH JUICE RESERVED
	● HOT PEPPER SAUCE

Cocktail Sauce

This cocktail sauce has a fresher, sharper taste than the commercial ones. Serve it with raw oysters on the half shell or fried oysters. It's an American classic.

1 Combine ketchup, tomato paste, lemon juice, horseradish, and hot pepper sauce in a serving bowl.

2 If possible, make 1 hour before serving and chill. Serve cold.

MAKES ¾ CUP

● ½ CUP TOMATO KETCHUP	● ⅛ TSP HOT PEPPER SAUCE
● 1 TBSP TOMATO PASTE	● FRIED OYSTERS (PAGE 133)
● 1 TSP LEMON JUICE	OR OYSTERS ON THE HALF
● 3 TBSP DRAINED PREPARED	SHELL
WHITE HORSERADISH	

Note

To open an oyster, use a short, thick-bladed knife; a brittle blade may snap and cause serious injury. Place a well-scrubbed oyster in a towel, with the deep part of the shell toward the palm. Work the knife into the shell, just to one side of the hinge, and ease it into the hinge. When shell feels loosened, run the knife along the top inside the shell to remove the top shell. Then run the knife under the oyster to release muscle and make the oyster easier for guests to eat.

Whole Wheat Puffs

• ¾ CUP WATER	• ¼ TSP SALT
• 6 TBSP BUTTER, CUT INTO	• 3 EGGS, AT ROOM
CHUNKS	TEMPERATURE
• ½ CUP ALL-PURPOSE FLOUR	
• ¼ CUP WHOLE WHEAT	
FLOUR	

Whole wheat flour gives these puffs a nutty taste. Make a thumb-nail-sized version, and serve plain as a snack.

1 Preheat oven to 375 degrees. Grease and flour a cookie sheet. Combine water and butter in a saucepan and bring to a boil.

2 Meanwhile, stir flours together with salt and have ready. When water is at full boil, stir in flour mixture all at once and reduce heat to low. Stir constantly until dough comes together in a smooth ball. Remove from heat and cool 5 minutes. Beat in eggs, one at a time, incorporating first before adding second.

3 Drop mixture by heaping tablespoons about 2 inches apart onto cookie sheet. Bake in oven about 30 minutes, or until golden brown. Turn off heat and allow to cool in oven 10 minutes. Remove from oven and cool.

4 Carefully slice each puff horizontally in half. Pull out any wet dough inside and allow puffs to dry completely. Fill just before serving.

MAKES 18 TO 20 PUFFS

Note

Puffs can be stored at room temperature for a few hours. For long-term storage, wrap carefully and freeze.

HAPPY ENDINGS

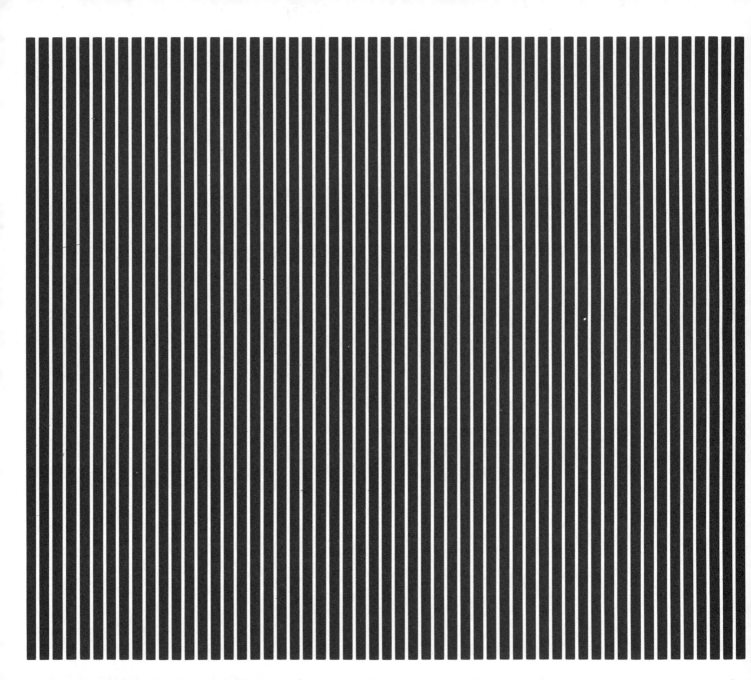

ne perfect Chocolate Truffle with Hazelnut Liqueur will close any party on a sweet note.

Make extras. You'll find guests eager to "take some home to the children."

Chocolate Truffles with Hazelnut Liqueur

● 2½ OZ (⅓ CUP) HAZELNUT LIQUEUR	● 12 OZ MILK CHOCOLATE
	● 10 OZ SEMISWEET CHOCOLATE
● ½ CUP HEAVY CREAM	
● 7 TBSP BUTTER	● COCOA

These are the perfect way to signal guests that the party has been sweet but that it's time to leave.

1 Pour hazelnut liqueur into a small saucepan. Bring to a boil and simmer until liqueur is reduced by one half. Remove from heat and add cream, 3 tablespoons butter, and milk chocolate. Place pan over another pan filled with simmering water and allow chocolate to melt, stirring often. When chocolate has melted and reached 110 degrees, remove from heat. Pour chocolate into a bowl and refrigerate until firm, several hours.

2 When chocolate is firm, remove from refrigerator and shape about 2 teaspoons of chocolate into a small ball. Repeat until all chocolate is used. Work quickly and don't handle the chocolate too much since the heat from handling will melt it. Place the balls on a waxed paper-lined dish and freeze for several hours.

3 In the top of a double boiler, melt the semisweet chocolate and remaining 4 tablespoons butter. When chocolate reaches 110 degrees, remove from heat and, stirring often, allow to cool to 90 degrees. Remove chocolate balls from freezer and place, one at a time, in melted chocolate. Turn to cover each ball and then place on waxed paper-lined dish. Sprinkle with sifted cocoa. Truffles will harden at room temperature. Serve cool.

SERVES 28

REFERENCE
TABLES

T he following are conversion tables and other information applicable to those converting the recipes in this book for use in other English-speaking countries. The cup and spoon measures given in this book are U.S. Customary; use these tables when working with British Imperial or Metric kitchen utensils.

Liquid Measures

The old Imperial pint is larger than the U.S. pint; therefore note the following when measuring the liquid ingredients.

U.S.	IMPERIAL
1 CUP = 8 FLUID OUNCES	1 CUP = 10 FLUID OUNCES
½ CUP = 4 FLUID OUNCES	½ CUP = 5 FLUID OUNCES
1 TABLESPOON = ¾ FLUID OUNCE	1 TABLESPOON = 1 FLUID OUNCE

U.S. MEASURE	METRIC	IMPERIAL*	
1 QUART	946 ML	1½+	PINTS
1 PINT	473 ML	¾+	PINT
1 CUP	236 ML	−½	PINT
1 TABLESPOON	15 ML	−1	TABLESPOON
1 TEASPOON	5 ML	−1	TEASPOON

*Note that exact quantities cannot always be given. Differences are more crucial when dealing with larger quantities. For teaspoon and tablespoon measures, simply use scant quantities, or for more accurate conversions rely upon metric measures.

Weight and Volume Measures

U.S. cooking procedures usually measure certain items by volume, although in the Metric or Imperial systems they are measured by weight. Here are some approximate equivalents for basic items.*

	U.S. CUSTOMARY	METRIC	IMPERIAL
APPLES (PEELED AND SLICED)	3 CUPS	500 G	1 POUND
BEANS, DRIED (RAW)	2½ CUPS	450 G	1 POUND
BUTTER	1 CUP	250 G	8 OUNCES
	½ CUP	125 G	4 OUNCES
	¼ CUP	62 G	2 OUNCES
	1 TABLESPOON	15 G	½ OUNCE
CHEESE (GRATED)	½ CUP	60 G	2 OUNCES
CORNSTARCH	1 TEASPOON	10 G	⅓ OUNCE
CREAM OF TARTAR	1 TEASPOON	3-4 G	⅛ OUNCE
FLOUR, ALL-PURPOSE	1 CUP	128 G	4¼ OUNCES
(SIFTED)	½ CUP	60 G	2⅛ OUNCES
	¼ CUP	32 G	1 OUNCE
HERBS, FRESH	¼ CUP WHOLE	15 G	½ OUNCE
	2 TABLESPOONS CHOPPED	7 G	¼ OUNCE
MUSHROOMS, FRESH (CHOPPED)	4 CUPS	300 G	10 OUNCES
NUT MEATS	1 CUP	112 G	4 OUNCES
PEAS, FRESH (SHELLED)	1 CUP	450 G	1 POUND
POTATOES (MASHED)	2 CUPS	450 G	1 POUND
RAISINS (OR SULTANAS)	¾ CUP	125 G	4 OUNCES
RICE	1 CUP (RAW)	225 G	8 OUNCES
	3 CUPS (COOKED)	225 G	8 OUNCES
SPINACH, FRESH (COOKED)	½ CUP	285 G	10 OUNCES

*So as to avoid awkward measurements, some conversions are not exact.

	U.S. CUSTOMARY	METRIC	IMPERIAL
SUGAR:	1 CUP	240 G	8 OUNCES
GRANULATED	½ CUP	120 G	4 OUNCES
	¼ CUP	60 G	2 OUNCES
	1 TABLESPOON	15 G	½ OUNCE
CONFECTIONERS'	1 CUP	140 G	5 OUNCES
	½ CUP	70 G	3 OUNCES
	¼ CUP	35 G	1+ OUNCE
	1 TABLESPOON	10 G	¼ OUNCE
BROWN	1 CUP	160 G	5⅓ OUNCES
	½ CUP	80 G	2⅔ OUNCES
	¼ CUP	40 G	1⅓ OUNCES
	1 TABLESPOON	10 G	⅓ OUNCE
TOMATOES, FRESH (PEELED, SEEDED, JUICED)	1½ CUPS	450 G	1 POUND
ZUCCHINI	3½ CUPS (SLICED)	450 G	1 POUND
	2 CUPS (GRATED)	450 G	1 POUND

Oven Temperatures

GAS MARK	¼	2	4	6	8
FAHRENHEIT	225	300	350	400	450
CELSIUS	107	150	178	205	233

American Cooking Equivalents

1 TEASPOON = ⅓ TABLESPOON

1 TABLESPOON = 3 TEASPOONS

2 TABLESPOONS = 1 FLUID OUNCE

4 TABLESPOONS = ¼ CUP OR 2 OUNCES

5⅓ TABLESPOONS = ⅓ CUP OR 2⅔ OUNCES

8 TABLESPOONS = ½ CUP OR 4 OUNCES

16 TABLESPOONS = 1 CUP OR 8 OUNCES

¼ CUP = 4 TABLESPOONS

1 CUP = ½ PINT OR 8 FLUID OUNCES

2 CUPS = 1 PINT OR 16 FLUID OUNCES

1 QUART (LIQUID) = 2 PINTS OR 4 CUPS

1 GALLON (LIQUID) = 4 QUARTS

Glassware for Cocktails

MARTINI   STEMMED MUG   OLD-FASHIONED   TOM COLLINS   HIGHBALL   SOUR   PILSNER

Glassware
for Champagne, Wine,
and Cordials

CHAMPAGNE FLUTE   CHAMPAGNE SAUCER   WHITE WINE   RED WINE   BRANDY SNIFTER   CORDIAL

Index

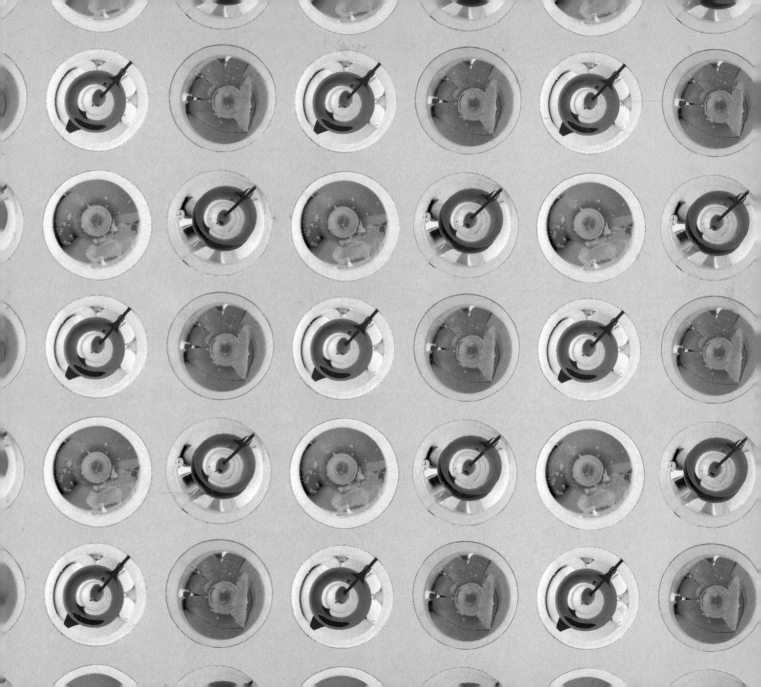